A Systematic Guide to Change Management

Best Practice in Leading Change and Influencing Stakeholders

by

Ken Thompson

with introduction by

Charles Spinosa

July 2016
Revision: 1.03

NEW CHAPTER ADDED JANUARY 2018:
Influencing communities: leading large-scale change in the digital era

*A Systematic Introduction to
Change Management*

Except as provided by the Copyright Act 1968, no part of this publication may be reproduced, stored in any retrieval system or transmitted in any form or by any means without the prior written permission of the authors.
All rights reserved.

A Systematic Introduction to Change Management

A Systematic Introduction to Change Management

Although Ken Thompson brilliantly and quickly summarizes the best of the best change-management thinkers, John Kotter, Robert Kaplan and David Norton, Jeannie Daniel Duck, Robert H. Schaffer and Harvey A. Thomson, and Mark Hughes, this book is no simple epitome of the best thinking in change management. Ken Thompson is changing change management. He is one of the leading-edge practitioner-thinkers who is carefully evolving change management from a planning discipline into a political one.

CHARLES SPINOSA, Ph.D., Group Director & Leader, Strategy and Customer Experience VISION Consulting

Ken has written a succinct yet powerful summary of change management thinking, approaches and tools, presented in a practical and accessible manner. Excellent reading for anyone involved with the leadership and management of change.

CHRIS COLLISON, Author and Former Director of Change and Knowledge Management, Centrica.

This is a must-read for anyone who is involved in leading or helping to champion any organizational change initiative. The guide is full of really useful frameworks, practical tips and pitfalls to avoid. It would take a long time to research all of these dimensions of change management but Ken Thompson manages to compress it all neatly into a very easy-to-read mini bible. There are also plenty of useful references for any readers who want to go further into any of the topics. It will be on my shelf as a go-to guide for the future.

NOEL CLERKIN, Senior Principal Consultant at Axialent - improving individual, team and organizational performance.

A Systematic Introduction to Change Management

Ken Thompson applies his established system thinking expertise to produce a holistic appraisal of best practices in change management backed up with case studies and exercises. If you need a clear, concise and informed approach to change management whilst equipping yourself with the tools to make it work, this is the book for you.

SIMON SCHOLFIELD, System Dynamics expert for the Dow Chemical company.

Ken Thompson has done a fantastic job of pulling together the know-how you can leverage on for systematically driving your change management initiatives. The shared insights and clarity of message are as impressive as the bucket-load of tools provided. Read this book to get a solid overview on change management and you will have a wealth of insights to propel your own activities forward.

PIERRE WETTERGREN, CEO Clever Collaboration Group and winner of "Security Consultant of the year 2013".

A fantastic and accessibly written book which uses a variety of unique metaphors and examples to bring change management to life. The power of mindset during times of change is appropriately highlighted and there are exercises to encourage direct application throughout. I have used Ken's computer-based change simulation many times and it is an excellent tool to engage people and allow them to receive instant feedback on their change management decisions!

MELANIE WALLINGER, Consultant and Occupational Psychologist.

A Systematic Introduction to Change Management

This book is very useful in any leader's toolbox. It's full of well researched and expertly presented ideas, all of which are backed up by real life applications that are both are practical and hands on. Ken demonstrates his astute understanding of Change Management in a straightforward and actionable way. A great read!

DARRAGH MCGILLICUDDY, MD at McGillicuddy Consulting.

A Systematic Introduction to Change Management

Table of Contents

About the Authors 8
INTRODUCTION by Charles Spinosa 13
   Changing Change Management 13
   Itinerary..14
   The Goal of Seeing Change Management as Politics 15
   Change Management as Planning 16
   Change Management as Politics...18
   Is Change Management as Politics Good? 20
WHAT IS CHANGE MANAGEMENT, REALLY? 22
   The Political Model of Change 22
   The Biological Model of Change...24
   Do 70% of all change initiatives really fail? 26
   Change programs need balanced scorecards 27
   The most obvious change management mistakes to avoid ...30
   Expect your change management program to succeed..........31
CORE PRINCIPLES OF CHANGE MANAGEMENT..................35
   Principle 1: What's the Story of the Change? 36
   Principle 2: Have a Change Plan 36
   Principle 3: Never fly blind...37
   Principle 4: Measure twice — cut once... 38
   Principle 5: Round up your supporters... 39
   Principle 6: ...But don't ignore powerful opponents... 40
   Principle 7: Influence the Influential ... .41
   Principle 8: If you can't be direct, then be indirect 42
   Principle 9: Don't forget those who helped get you started.42
   Principle 10: Rome was not built in a day... 43
   Principle 11: Expect unexpected change! 44
   Principle 12: Finally, ...rip up that change cookbook... 45
CHANGE MANAGEMENT BASICS..47
   Change Models..47
   Change Narratives..51
   Change Planning..54
CHANGE MANAGEMENT TECHNIQUES 57
   3 Principles for Engaging Individuals 57
   Change Engagement Model 58
   Selecting appropriate interventions 61

*A Systematic Introduction to
Change Management*

CHANGE MANAGEMENT TOOLS 67
   SNA: Social Network Analysis 68
   DICE: A Change Risk Assessment Technique 71
   RIVER DIAGRAM: Community Change Visualisation 76
   COHORT: Change Simulation Game 80
   SPREAD: Community Change Simulation 83
INFLUENCING COMMUNITIES: LEADING LARGE-SCALE
CHANGE IN THE DIGITAL ERA 87
   Setting the scene 87
   The difference between a community and a crowd - and why
   it matters 89
   The role of super-connectors in mass change 91
   Key types of activity you need in your change campaign 93
   Risks of email and social media in mass change 98
   Best practices in individual and mass persuasion 100
   Tips for successfully managing large-scale community change
   109
   Chapter References & Further Reading 111
CHANGE MANAGEMENT CASE STUDIES 112
   Y2K (The Millennium Bug) 113
   The Good Friday Agreement (N. Ireland Peace Process) 115
   Smoking in Public Places (England) 117
   JC Penney 119
   Ford Motor Company 121
   5 Featured Change Projects: Perspectives 123
   Other Major Change Projects 128
SELECT READING LIST ON CHANGE 131
APPENDICES 132
   Appendix 1: Introduction to Business Cases 133
   Appendix 2: Lite Framework for Change Mgt. 137
   Appendix 3: TechVet Company Briefing 140
   Appendix 4: High Performing Teams in a hurry! 145
INDEX 152

A Systematic Introduction to Change Management

About the Authors

The book is authored by Ken Thompson, an expert practitioner, author and speaker on collaboration, high performing teams, change management, game-based learning, experiential learning and social learning.

Ken has written seven books and his work has featured in major publications including The Guardian Newspaper, Wired Magazine, The Huffington Post and The Henry Ford Magazine.

Ken has also spoken at a number of international events including TEDx, the Institute for Healthcare Improvement (IHI) and NASA conferences.

Ken is delighted and honoured that long-time colleague and frequent mentor, Charles Spinosa, generously agreed to write an introductory chapter. Charles is one of the world's most insightful thinker/practitioners on engaging people through real conversations which is a core theme of the book.

Charles Spinosa, Ph.D., is a Group Director at VISION Consulting. For the last 20 years, Charles Spinosa has helped clients create cultural innovations, which are new ways of doing things that overcome value conflicts between businesses and their customers or in the customer's own lives. These cultural innovations drive profitable increases in market share, share of wallet, entry into new markets. Charles leads VISION's research work in strategy, organization behavior, and customer experience.

Charles's recent publications are: with Hancocks and Glennon, "Coping with time in organizations,"

A Systematic Introduction to Change Management

Perspectives on Process Organization Studies, volume 7 (forthcoming); with Davis and Glennon, "Transforming Crippling Company Politics," Organizational Dynamics (2014); with Glennon and Sota, "The Virtues of the Transformational Leader," Business Strategy Review (2008); and with Sull, "Promise-based Management," HBR (2007).

A Systematic Introduction to Change Management

The Systematic Guides Series

Systematic Guides are aimed at leaders and managers who need to instantly access 'Organization-Ready' models, practices, checklists and guidance in key subject areas which are logically organized and based on best practice.

Each Systematic Guide references online team-based business simulation games, designed by the author, which provide powerful experiential and social learning tools for rapidly bringing each book's content to life in a fun and engaging way.

This guide provides a pragmatic framework for the interventions needed to successfully identify and intervene with key stakeholders in a Change Management project with the objective of winning their support and commitment.

The guide starts by reviewing some of the latest thinking on change and, based on this, proposes a set of guiding principles for change management.

The guide offers concise guidance on change management interventions with individuals, teams and groups and offers clear instructions and tips on when and how best to employ. The guide also provides useful material on different Change 'models' and how to create a compelling 'Change Narrative'.

For change to make a real impact it must go beyond small groups of leaders and extend into the bigger front-line communities who these leaders are responsible for or whom they serve as suppliers and business partners. This requires change managers and change leaders to be adept

*A Systematic Introduction to
Change Management*

at bringing about change by Influencing Communities (and Crowds) both internal and external.

The guide dedicates a chapter to the key challenges in influencing communities in our always-on, electronically-mediated and hyper-connected world and proposes a set of practical insights and techniques for succeeding in this challenging area.

The guide concludes with a chapter on Change Management Case Studies.

*A Systematic Introduction to
Change Management*

There are 5 books in the Systematic Guides series:

VOLUME 1: A Systematic Guide to High Performing Teams (HPTs), Ken Thompson, December 2015

VOLUME 2: A Systematic Guide to Game-Based Learning (GBL) in Organizational Teams, Ken Thompson, January 2016

VOLUME 3: A Systematic Guide to Business Acumen and Leadership using Dilemmas, Ken Thompson, February 2016

VOLUME 4: A Systematic Guide to Change Management, Ken Thompson, July 2016

VOLUME 5: A Systematic Guide to Collaboration and Competition in Organizations, Ken Thompson, March 2017

A Systematic Introduction to Change Management

INTRODUCTION by Charles Spinosa

Changing Change Management

Although Ken Thompson brilliantly and quickly summarizes the best of the best change-management thinkers, John Kotter, Robert Kaplan and David Norton, Jeannie Daniel Duck, Robert H. Schaffer and Harvey A. Thomson, and Mark Hughes, this book is no simple epitome of the best thinking in change management. Ken Thompson is changing change management. He is one of the leading-edge practitioner-thinkers who is carefully evolving change management from a planning discipline into a political one.

I suspect that Ken is one of the first to see the importance of the political dimension because he lives in Northern Ireland where over the course of his life, he has witnessed intense, brilliant, risky, and successful political change management. However, other forward-looking thinkers have come to similar positions. The Australian practitioner-scholar Brad Rolfe thinks in Ken's direction. Others talk about constant persuasion. Still, it is a bit surprising that the full political dimension of change management has not come out even more strongly across the wider change community.

Standing back from the details of change management programs and looking broadly at changes in competition over the past decade, we can easily see that we are in an age of global networks, alliances, collective strategies, and outsourcing. Government regulation mounts. How many change managers today could be lucky enough to run a change management program that affected only internal staff? Such a program would surely be a rare bird and likely already extinct in many industries. Today's change

A Systematic Introduction to Change Management

leaders have constantly to negotiate with at least multiple suppliers, outsourcers, and communities of customers. In at least a handful of important industries, add regulators to the list.

This movement towards increasing regulation, drawing on global supply chains, and dis-integrating organizations may explain a further observation. Though few are writing about change management as centrally political, the basic claim of this book--that change management is politics by other means--is widely held among successful practitioners. They concede Ken's point but prefer to talk about planning. To some extent Ken Thompson continues the tradition. He gives full voice to politics at the beginning of this book but its role remains a little more subtle as he summarizes the best of the best thinking. He does return to politics at the end in two of his five signal cases of recent change management: The Good Friday Agreement (Northern Ireland Peace Process) and Smoking in Public Places (England).

Itinerary

Having worked with Ken on numerous change projects, I believe that the most useful introduction I can give to this book will be to set out the goal of emphasizing the political dimension of change management, say what change management looks like in going from the planning to the political orientation, point out some of the places where the political dimension comes out most vividly in the book, and finally say something about the implications of this shift in orientation and why it is for the good.

A Systematic Introduction to Change Management

One small note before turning to Ken's goal. For some, politics has a bad name. It suggests shady dealings. There are certainly bad politics. Ken, however, writes about good politics, how we come to agreement when there is no capacity or time to think everything through. Ken's is the politics of persuasion, not coercion. His key tool is using multiple routes to influence, understanding your audience and finding the right spokesperson or group. He pretty much ignores the much used, old-fashioned tool of making organizational change happen: displacing or terminating opponents to change. Again, we may have the hard-won lessons of Northern Ireland to thank for that Ken's pacific tone.

The Goal of Seeing Change Management as Politics

What is Ken's goal of reorienting change management from planning to politics? For years, the business thinkers have complained that 70% of change projects never lived up to their promise. Ken goes through the studies that show that the 70% was always too high a figure. He quite rightly says that change projects are increasingly making the change promised and doing so more or less on time and with the expected budget. However, they are doing that because change managers have become ever more astute at managing the politics of multiple stakeholders. The goal of the emphasizing the politics is to make change management work better at achieving what it has always set out to do: complete a significant change in the way an organization works with a specified budget and within a specified time. He is not overturning the aspirations of planners at all.

A Systematic Introduction to Change Management

Change Management as Planning

As practiced across the many, different change management frameworks, planners thought that change started with a vision of the future state and the basic change in operations that had to take place to get there. As its motivation, change worked best with a burning platform and second best with a golden opportunity. But the minute after the lightning vision has struck, change managers donned on their change management gear and become first requirement gatherers. Their teams interviewed stakeholders for the requirements of the new vision. At best, a stage of ingenious simplification followed with careful negation of the simplification across stakeholders.

After that, the change manager carefully worked out a plan with multiple work streams. The best plans would break the whole program of work into bite-sized modules each of whose successful completion, measured according to a Kaplan-Norton balanced scorecard, called for organization-wide celebration. Modules were frequently iterative, the change agent would get a new process up and running with some ad hoc support so that lessons could be learned and adjustments made in the next module which refined and completed the earlier one. Nevertheless, the change manager identified critical paths and made sure that work streams converged at the right times. Achieving such a convergence successfully demonstrates both yesterday and today an enormous level of craft.

The accomplished change manager looked at both personal transformation and operational, process, or system change and set goals for both. In order to keep stakeholders involved ("at bay" would be more apt), governance meetings were meticulously planned. Finally,

A Systematic Introduction to Change Management

with so much planning, the costs of the teams and supplies emerged, and as a final act of meticulousness and wide-ranging vision, the change manager set out the business case consisting of a vision + summary of the plan + cost + estimated financial benefit, and concluded with the return on investment.

Upon approval, the change manager drove the plan forward as hard as possible forcing individual project managers and teams to make simple, necessary adjustments fast. The change manager coordinated all these simple adjustments and adjusted the plan accordingly to keep to the planned cost and time. When simple adjustments did not suffice in the face of resistance, changed circumstances, or insufficiently-thought-through solutions, then the change manager would propose change orders. (Leave aside the checkered past of change orders. In principle, no planner can ever anticipate every untoward contingency.)

Traditionally, the change manager did not promise to deliver the magic of the change. That was up to the people operating under the changed way of working. The change manager simply promised the creation of the plan and then the steady implementation of it with adjustments according to the recommendations of the governance committee. Frequently no one took full and direct responsibility for making the change happen. The leader who granted the funds might have had full but no direct responsibility. Direct responsibility for the magic of the claim resided, like some titles to land under the old law of trust, in the clouds.

A Systematic Introduction to Change Management

Change Management as Politics

This cloudy responsibility brings us to the first political practice Ken insists that change managers master. He summarizes it in the jargon of test-pilot astronauts, "Failure is not an option." Unlike almost all business and life today, change management does not reside in a world of options. Change managers stand on burning platforms organizing teams to achieve the golden opportunity of their lifetimes.

In the world of the change manager, there is simply nothing else for them to do, and there is nothing else that they would rather do. In short, the change becomes a mission. It is a political mission because its goal is to convert the hearts and minds of those who will enact and work under the change. That does not mean that the successful change manager is a spin doctor. The change manager takes responsibility for making the change happen and happening meaningfully for the stakeholders. Some stakeholders will care about profits. Some will care about customer satisfaction. Some will care about operational simplicity. Many who report directly to the change manager will care about fulfilling the vision of the plan. The change manager has to make the palatable for all constituencies and get, as Ken tells us, 95% on board.

This political view of change management does not deny the planning approach as much as displace it. Of Ken's twelve core principles four, including the great story of change, summarize the planning approach. Eight of his core principles are about political management. Even principles like "never fly blind" and "measure twice—cut once," which seem to be about regular publication of operational measures, are instead about knowing your stakeholders' "commitments, ambitions, status, and

*A Systematic Introduction to
Change Management*

history," on the one hand, and measuring the influence and attitude of each stakeholder, on the other.
What do the eight political principles entail? What, in short, is the core job of the change manager? Today's political change manager stands for the magic of the change and does so by constant conversations—think campaign stops—with constituents.

The change manager divides constituents into early supporters, recent supporters, influential supporters, and influential opponents. A political change manager then holds conversations to keep the excitement of the change in the hearts and minds of the early, new, and influential supporters. That manager figures out who or which group is best to influence each powerful opponent. The manager works hard to design those conversations so that they always address the opponents' "commitments, ambitions, status, and histories."

It may seem nearly impossible that a change manager can be both a brilliant planner and politician. These are skills that require constant practice. Fortunately, our online world gives change managers online simulations that they can use to keep their conversational strategy and design skills sharp. Like pilots, who then can get inside a safe simulator and practice, practice, practice, Ken calls out COHORT and SPREAD as his favored simulators.

The political change manager has a wider remit and wider responsibility than the planning change manager. Many change programs failed to achieve their goals because various stakeholders in and outside the organization simply lost interest. Teams reporting to them became sluggish or looked to find positions outside the change program. Today's political change managers have constantly to reinspire those who are losing faith.

A Systematic Introduction to Change Management

"Failure is not an option." Today's political change manager also has to note when a program comes under threat because of a significant change in customer taste, technology, or regulation. The political change manager then works closely with the visionary behind the change to change the change itself. The political change manager promises to effect the change and deliver its anticipated benefits.

Is Change Management as Politics Good?

So far as this new breed of change managers drives higher rates of success, the change in change management is clearly good for the profession. Is it good for business and life more broadly? Much in industry in the last century focused on rationalized standardization of products, operations, management, and therefore of life itself. Recipes and routine ruled.

Two different roles emerged. The thinker came up with the recipe for the product, management, the organization, or the change. Then the doer followed the recipe meticulously and with force. Though useful for getting an amazing array of products to millions of consumers, the distinction was always artificial. Doers always had to make adjustments that went outside the frame of the recipe either for making the organization and its culture or for making the product. Entrepreneurs and other successful leaders always kept their hands and eyes in the doing, because that is where the insights came from.

The planning change manager was first a thinker and then a doer. The political change manager closes the gap between thinking and doing in constantly promoting and rethinking the vision of the change while moving it forward. Thus, change management as politics is an

A Systematic Introduction to Change Management

important piece of culture work for us today. If it succeeds, all workers will move closer to becoming thinking doers and hence have a materially and ethically richer life. We will then have good reason to thank practitioner-thinkers like Ken Thompson who are playing their part in making this culture change happen.

*A Systematic Introduction to
Change Management*

WHAT IS CHANGE MANAGEMENT, REALLY?

The Political Model of Change

With the impressive array of frameworks, techniques, checklists, models, business cases and tools which support change management it is very easy to 'miss the wood for the trees'.

Right from the outset I contend that first and foremost Change Management is a Political Campaign within an organization with lots of other supporting activities 'tacked on'. If you mismanage this political campaign, then it does not matter very much how well you do all or any of the other things – they will be mere window dressing on a failed change!

What do I mean by a 'Political Campaign'?

To bring about a new government in a country, a party or coalition need to win sufficient support for what they stand for and promise to do with the people of that country. To bring about change in an organization you need to win sufficient support for the promise of the change with the people of that organization. This means people at all levels in the organization including the people at the top, often referred to as 'Stakeholders', middle management and the rest of the people whose day to day working lives will either be improved, left unaltered or negatively impacted by the change.

If you were leading a political party seeking re-election you would have limited resources so you would have to decide how to communicate your message to maximum effect. So you might identify key influencers within your target

A Systematic Introduction to Change Management

community and see if you could win their support in partnering with you to spread your message. You might also identify influential people who could hinder your messaging and at very least see if you can moderate their opposition in some way. If you are wise you might also make sure that you and your team are not just spreading your message but also listening to the concerns raised by the voters and then thinking about whether your message is hitting the mark and where it might need to be changed.

You would also develop a strategy for your different communication channels such as mass communications, town hall meetings and one to one communications on people doorsteps. Likewise, you would also decide what documents and other media artifacts such as posters and videos you would need to support your campaign.

The exact same rationale applies to organizational change. You need to communicate your message effectively with the right balance between the influential and the man on the 'shop floor' (who may have concerns which the influential have totally missed). You need to be listening to the concerns of the people you communicate with and make sure there are no relationship issues or other baggage getting in the way before you launch into your change story.

You need to decide the best way to engage with the people of the organization and where you should meet with large groups, small groups and individuals. You also need to decide on the documents and other artifacts you develop to support your campaign.

This is what I mean when I say that change management is not primarily a project to be managed with activities and tasks and deliverables but rather a political campaign of story-telling, listening and persuasion with the aim of building a following of sufficient scale within the company so that the change takes hold and improves the fortunes of the company and the lives of those who work in it.

Also please let me very be clear what I don't mean by 'political'. I am not referring to what is commonly called 'organizational or office politics' where people back-stab, misrepresent and form informal alliances to promote their own careers and agendas in an organization. Such behavior does not contribute to the successful implementation of change in any organization.

The Biological Model of Change

In 2008, I wrote a book titled 'Bioteams - High Performance Teams Based on Nature's Most Successful Designs' where I looked to nature for some radically different models for teams and groups within organizations. In technical terms, this subject is known as 'organizational biomimicry'.

One of the writers who I found both helpful and personally encouraging at the time was Fritjof Capra an Austrian-born American physicist who takes a very broad and holistic view of both science and life.

Fritjof, in his excellent and wide-ranging book, The Hidden Connections, [1] eloquently argues the case that 'social systems' such as organizations and networks, are not just like living systems, they are living systems! Capra describes five metaphors that people have used to understand organizations: machines, organisms, brains, cultures and systems of government. He concludes that the fundamental debate is really whether we see our organizations as Machines (predictable) or Living Systems (unpredictable).

A Systematic Introduction to Change Management

Simplifying Capra's argument slightly, I would suggest that there are really two competing mindsets in the way people think of organizational change – 'clocks' or 'cells'. If we have a 'clock mindset' we view our organization as a machine which can be maintained, repaired and improved on a pretty predictable basis. Alternatively, if we have a 'cell mind-set' then to us an organization is more a living thing where despite the inputs we might make, which may have worked before, the outcomes each time are largely unpredictable.

Do you have a clock or cell mindset about change? Most people are not at either extreme but somewhere on a spectrum between the two. The key distinction which I am proposing from the outset is that both mindsets have a valid place in change management and the ability to simultaneous consider both mindsets is, in fact, a critical skill for a successful change manager. Some aspects of a change can be quite controllable and predictable but others cannot. An intelligent change manager needs to live with this constant tension of 'clock vs cell' and to be able to plan and act accordingly. Your professional background might give you preferences one way or the other but you really need to embrace both mindsets to succeed.

According to ecologists, living systems cannot be 'managed' but rather they can only be 'perturbed' (a more scientific term for being disturbed). We should therefore not only think in terms of (predictable) change management but also in terms of (unpredictable) perturbation management.

Perturbation Management in essence simply means that, for certain aspects, you need to be prepared to try some things out first with your target change community in a controlled, experimental way. You then must review the results you get. If these results are heading in the broadly desired direction you need then do more of the same.

A Systematic Introduction to Change Management

Alternatively, if the results are heading in the wrong direction, then you need to stop doing what you are doing and do something different.

Ecologists also recognize two types of change in ecosystems and social systems such as organizations: [2]

- Type 1 – Progressive change due to internal self-organizing processes.
- Type 2 – Quantum change from one "stability domain" to another because of external disturbances.

So the role of an organizational change manager is really to act as a 'catalyst' to help the organization "jump" its operation and performance to a higher level stability domain through Type 2 change.

Do 70% of all change initiatives really fail?

Almost everyone who is involved in some way in the change management world will have come across the above statistic. However, if this is true then it is rather demoralizing for both change management professionals and senior executives who sponsor change management projects in their organizations. For Change Managers, it means that two out of three times they are failing in their professional jobs. For Business Sponsors, it means initiating a change management project is a pretty high-risk and career-limiting thing to consider.

Fortunately, however in recent years, people have started to question whether this statistic is based on real evidence. For example, Mark Hughes, from Brighton University, in an article in 2011 for The Journal of Change Management [3]. Hughes firstly identifies where this statistic actually originated, namely in generic statements made in the ground-breaking books of some of the top management pioneers of change management such as Michael Hammer and John Kotter, for example:

'Sadly, we must report that despite the success stories described in previous chapters, many companies that begin re-engineering don't succeed at it...Our <u>unscientific estimate</u> is that as many as 50 percent to 70 percent of the organizations that undertake a re-engineering effort do not achieve the dramatic results they intended.' (Michael Hammer 1993)

'From years of study, I <u>estimate</u> today more than 70 per cent of needed change either fails to be launched, even though some people clearly see the need, fails to be completed even though some people exhaust themselves trying, or finishes over budget, late and with initial aspirations unmet.' (John Kotter, 2008)

We should note that even the pioneers themselves make clear these comments are qualitative as opposed to quantitative. They are also US culture-centric and somewhat dated and also include projects which never even got started!

Hughes goes on to conclude in the paper that although Change Management can be very challenging, 70 % of all organizational change initiatives do <u>not</u> fail and it is quite meaningless to attempt to tag an activity so individual and complex as change management with such a simplistic and depressing collective failure rate.

Change programs need balanced scorecards

One of the main dilemmas encountered in any change management program is which results to 'steer' by to tell you how it is going. There are two main challenges – delays and fixation.

A Systematic Introduction to Change Management

Many results, typically financial, happen long after the activity which caused these results has ceased. These are referred to as 'lagging' indicators and are outcome measures. They are an essential business perspective as ultimately profits are what the business is there to generate. However, because they are lagging indicators they are not effective early warning indicators because by the time you see these indicators all the activities which could have influenced these indicators are over. Example lagging Indicators include Sales, Revenue, Costs and Profits.

Other results, typically non-financial, happen much in advance of the lagging indicators. These are referred to as 'leading' indicators and are activity measures. They are also an essential business perspective as they provide excellent early warning systems and can allow you to conduct a Root Cause Analysis of problems. However, because they are leading indicators they are not effective outcome measures and never tell the ultimate story of how a change to a business is doing in a way which would satisfy its investors. Example leading indicators include proposals made per month, exit rates of customers, customer satisfaction levels and employee retention levels.

If you take the analogy of an aircraft pilot — airspeed and estimated time of arrival are lagging indicators whereas engine temperatures, altitude and headings are leading indicators. One of the most common causes of airplane crashes is called CFIT (Controlled Flight Into Terrain) which means that pilots have flown a perfectly good plane into a hillside or the ground. How could this happen? One of the main reasons it could happen is that the pilots spot an issue, typically accompanied by a warning light, and fixate on this single issue at the expense of the other critical indicators such as airspeed and altitude.

A Systematic Introduction to Change Management

So to successfully manage a change project you will need to have a balance of leading and lagging indicators and to avoid fixation on any one or two indicators at the expense of the others. The approach I outline here is known as the Balanced Scorecard [4] approach to measurement developed by Robert Kaplan and David Norton. The Balanced Scorecard is regarded as one of the best-evidenced approaches to developing and executing strategy with a good set of case studies and benefits.

The Balanced Scorecard approach suggests that there are 4 key perspectives we should measure and track in terms of the outcome of our change project:

1. Financial
2. Customer
3. Process
4. Learning

The Financial perspective is generally a lagging or outcome class of measure which is driven by the other 3 perspectives, which are generally leading indicators.

Balanced Scorecards are constructed by interviewing senior members of the organization to identify candidate indicators. To narrow these indicators down to a practical scorecard there a number of scorecard best practices such as:

- 1 or 2 lagging measures for every strategic objective
- If we have a choice of more than 1 measure, we should use the one that best tracks and communicates the intent
- Not more than 25 measures per scorecard

The balanced scorecard approach can be used to assess a Change Management project in terms of the results it produces. This should be the primary method of assessing such a project.

However, we should not forget that a Change Project can (and should) also be measured using traditional project metrics such as budget, timescales, quality and deliverables. A guiding principle should be that we have definitely only won the *consolation prize* if our change project scores brilliantly on all of its project metrics but yet fails to deliver the business results across the 4 key aspects of the Balanced Scorecard.

The most obvious change management mistakes to avoid

John Kotter, of the Harvard Business School, in his best-selling book 'Leading Change' [5] identifies 8 'errors' which result in the failure of organizational change programmes:

- Allowing too much complacency
- Failing to create a sufficiently powerful guiding coalition
- Underestimating the power of vision
- Under-communicating the vision by a factor of 10 (or more)
- Permitting obstacles to block the new vision
- Failing to create short-term wins
- Declaring victory too soon
- Neglecting to anchor changes firmly in the corporate culture

A Systematic Introduction to Change Management

Robert Schafer and Harvey Thompson, in an article [6] for the Harvard Business Review book 'On Change,' suggest that another major mistake is to focus on activity-based change management programs rather than results-based programs.

The authors suggest that there are 6 reasons 'why the cards are stacked against activity-centered improvement programs':

- Not keyed to specific results
- Too large scale and too diffused
- Results is a four letter word (not wanting to be seen as 'short-termist')
- Delusional Measurements (irrelevant or trivial indicators of success)
- Staff and Consultant-Driven
- Bias to Orthodoxy (no real learning)

Expect your change management program to succeed

Change Management success is neither easy nor trivial nor guaranteed, but it is not impossible either!

You only have to look around you to see successful change management projects on all scales – personal, family, business, community, country and internationally. We read all the time of successful business change projects, such as new company launches and mergers. We read all the time about successful national change projects too, such as the ongoing peace process in Northern Ireland and the changing of public attitudes and practices to smoking in public places (see later chapter on major Change Management Case Studies).

A Systematic Introduction to Change Management

If you take seriously the lessons in this mini-guide – building a strong narrative, having the right mindset, creating a balanced scorecard, developing a pragmatic plan and making the sensitively right interventions with the right people at the right time – then your change management project will succeed. Finally, it is my personal view that one of the biggest drivers of change management success is adopting the attitude embodied by NASA and demonstrated so powerfully in the film Apollo 13. When the stakes are high (and if they are not then why bother?) then failure should not be an option!

A Systematic Introduction to Change Management

Points for Reflection

1. What is your experience of change programmes where the political side has been neglected or the technical side over-emphasized?

2. Compare a recent change management programme with a recent political campaign. What insights does it give you as to what could have been done better in the organization?

3. Where do you sit on the cells versus clocks mindset of change management?

4. How would you measure the success of a change management program you have been involved in? What would be the key success indicators? How well do your indicators cover the Financial, Customer, Process and Learning aspects of business success?

5. How successful was this change program considered at the time, how successful is it considered now and how successful is it measured against your key indicators?

6. What have been the most common mistakes you have encountered in change management projects and what could be done to eliminate these mistakes?

A Systematic Introduction to Change Management

Chapter References

1. *The Hidden Connections*, Fritjof Capra, Flamingo, 2003.
2. *Human Ecology – Basic concepts for sustainable development*, Gerald Marten, Earthscan, 2003.
3. *Do 70 Per Cent of All Organizational Change Initiatives Really Fail?* Mark Hughes, The Journal of Change Management, 2011.
4. *The Balanced Scorecard,* Robert Kaplan and David Norton, Harvard Business Review Press, 1996.
5. *Leading Change: Why Transformation Efforts Fail,* John P Kotter, Harvard Business School Press, 1996.
6. *Successful Change Programmes begin with results*, Robert Schafer and Harvey Thompson, Harvard Business School Press, 1992.

A Systematic Introduction to Change Management

CORE PRINCIPLES OF CHANGE MANAGEMENT

In this chapter, by way of a foundation and an introduction, I have attempted to pull together 12 core principles of effective change management from my own experience and using best practice as recorded in the change management literature.

The 12 core principles are:

1. What's the Story of the Change?
2. Have a Change Plan
3. Never fly blind
4. Measure twice — cut once
5. Round up your supporters
6. But don't ignore powerful opponents
7. Influence the Influential
8. If you can't be direct, then be indirect
9. Don't forget those you helped get you started
10. Rome was not built in a day
11. Expect unexpected Change
12. Finally, rip up that Change cookbook

Let's explore each of the principles in a bit more detail.

A Systematic Introduction to Change Management

Principle 1: What's the Story of the Change?
You need a credible 'change narrative' which resonates with colleagues at all levels.

Carolyn Aiken and Scott Keller in an article [1] for *The McKinsey Quarterly*, argue that we need to have both 'burning platform' and 'missed opportunity' elements to our change narrative.

'It takes a story with both + and − to create real energy. The "deficit based" approach has become the model predominantly taught in business schools and is presumably the default change model in most organizations. Research has shown, however, that a story focused on what's wrong invokes blame and creates fatigue and resistance, doing little to engage people's passion and experience'... 'While it is impossible to prescribe generally how the divide should be split between positive and negative messages (as it will be specific to the context of any given change program), we strongly advise managers not to swing the pendulum too far in one direction or another'.

We cover change narratives in more detail in the next chapter.

Principle 2: Have a Change Plan
You <u>should</u> have a change plan or at very least some change goals.

Many of the problems identified earlier as the most common mistakes in change management programmes by

John Kotter [2] and others can be put down to lack of change planning.

Before we start our change program in earnest it makes sense to have honestly assessed the following:

- Have we the appetite to see this change through?
- Can we afford the money and resources to do the change job properly at this point in time?
- Have we learned from our previous change failures?
- What is the risk we might just make things even worse?

In a section later on 'Change Planning' we discuss the need for a change plan and we also suggest a checklist you can use to help you — "The 9 Cs of Successful Change Planning."

Principle 3: Never fly blind...
Gather insight and build relationships <u>before</u> you make any interventions.

To help you establish rapport and relationship you first need to do your homework and find out as much as you can about your colleagues <u>before</u> you meet. These days you have absolutely no excuse with LinkedIn profiles and corporate social networks freely available. However, don't over rely on these as they can be heavily 'spun' — you should also talk to people's colleagues and former colleagues.

A Systematic Introduction to Change Management

To gain insight into individuals you should consider how your proposed change might impact on 4 key areas for these individuals – Commitments, Ambitions, Status and History, (CASH for short):

- *Commitments* — does the change potentially make it easier or harder for the individuals to deliver?
- *Ambitions* – does the change potentially further or threaten the individuals?
- *Status* – does the change potentially strengthen or weaken the individual's position?
- *History* – have the individuals had good or bad experiences previously with similar changes?

Principle 4: Measure twice — cut once...
Change is about the right interventions at the right time.

It seems almost too obvious to say that you should make appropriate interventions which are relevant to the individual's attitude and made at the right time. For example, it is generally not a great idea to ask someone who is currently an opponent of the change to become a champion for it. With some interventions you will only get one chance to have the conversation, so make sure you don't blow it by being impatient and getting your timing wrong and trying to force a key conversation at the wrong time.

We need to be very sensitive about intervening with people who are negative and therefore instead of a heavy conversation such as why don't they support you it is

A Systematic Introduction to Change Management

usually better to use 'light touch interventions' such as seeking their opinions and asking for their advice.

A very useful technique at the beginning of any change management program is to perform a **Stakeholder Analysis** on the key players who will be impacted by or have an impact on the change program. This involves constructing a simple 3x3 matrix showing Influence (*Organizational or Social*) on one axis and the stakeholder's attitude to the change (*Supporter, Neutral or Opponent*) on the other axis as shown in the figure:

A simple Stakeholder Map

We will discuss the two main types of organizational influence in much more detail later.

Principle 5: Round up your supporters...
Build your change platform around your influential supporters.

It is generally accepted change management best practice that you should try and build your initial platform for change around your most influential supporters and potential supporters.

Mark Murphy, writing in *Forbes Magazine* [3] in 2015, suggests you should 'forget about the *antagonists* at first and put the initial focus on your *champions*. Because if you start where you already have a strong base of support, your champions will spread that message throughout their vast networks, building the strong platform you need. And when the folks who want to bring you down see that big base of support behind you, it squashes their influence.'

Principle 6: ...But don't ignore powerful opponents...
Don't neglect high influence opponents who could sabotage the change.

In the 2015 book 'Organizational Change Management Strategies in Modern Business' [4] we are advised that *"opponents to a change initiative should be approached and used and their concerns taken as seriously as the perspectives of change supporters."*

This is particularly important if an opponent to the change has high hierarchical or social influence in the organization. Such people need to be engaged early for the simple reason that you will have to deal with these individuals in a sensitive and patient way. It might, therefore, take some time for you to get these individuals on your side – or at least get the individual beyond being an opponent to being a 'neutral.'

One interesting thing about influential opponents is that if they are properly engaged they could become your strongest and most powerful supporters. That stubborn streak which might make these individuals seem like a real pain now can become your biggest asset later when times get tough or change fatigue sets in and people start questioning the whole point of the change.

There is a very useful paper, The Nature of Opposition [5], on the management website changingminds.org which offers a very useful checklist for exploring what might be motivating someone who is opposed to a change in terms of their Drivers, Perceptions, Potential and Triggers.

Principle 7: Influence the Influential ...
Intervene with those who are influential — make these people your change champions.

If you discover that you have little or no influence with someone, then you are wasting both your time and theirs trying to intervene with the individual further about the proposed change. It could be that they are implacably opposed to this, or even any, change.

Generally, up to 5% of any group never adopt a change [6] – if you decide you are dealing with one of these 5%-ers then just move on. You have enough scope to succeed by concentrating on the other 95%.

Alternatively, it could be that you are just not the right person to engage with this individual on this change – in that case see principle 8.

There are two main types of influence in work situations: *organizational influence* and *social influence*.

Organizational influence depends on the person's position in the hierarchy or in a flat structure, their experience or length of service. Social influence depends on the person's reputation and the extent of their social network in the organization. For more on these two types of influence see later in the chapter on Change Management Techniques.

Principle 8: If you can't be direct, then be indirect ...
Don't neglect indirect interventions such as using colleagues and teams!

Sometimes you are not the best person to influence another. However, all is not lost provided you can influence someone else who in turn can influence them. There are different ways to achieve this.

For example, you might ask a colleague (or a senior leader) to see if they can influence the individual. Alternatively, if the individual is part of a team (or social group) which includes colleagues who are 'change supporters' then you might take advantage of the positive group dynamic to help you influence the individual as part of a group intervention.

Principle 9: Don't forget those who helped get you started
If you neglect your core supporters their commitment will drop.

Nobody likes being taken for granted or being neglected. Be careful not to forget about your early supporters or the reverse of your toughest opponent becoming your strongest supporter can occur – your strongest supporter turning against you.

A Systematic Introduction to Change Management

You should also be aware that people who have gone out on a limb for you may feel exposed and vulnerable and perhaps doubting whether they have done the right thing so may need your ongoing reassurance and appreciation.

Finally, being a change supporter or change champion does require some specific skills so you must always be prepared to help and coach people with what they are expected to do in this role. For more on 'Change Champions' see the chapter on Change Management Techniques.

Principle 10: Rome was not built in a day...
Be patient – change momentum sometimes builds very slowly.

In an excellent paper, *Understanding & Managing Reactions to Change* [6] by Gateshead Council, the authors suggest that:

'Sometimes we expect microwave results from a slow cooker. Sustainable change is never fast. It relies on exploring new ideas, new possibilities, listening, capturing potential and robust option appraisal'.

The authors go on to point out the real-world percentages about change management projects:

5% of people will lead the change

20% will get involved at the first opportunity

50% will wait and see what happens

20% will adopt when there is no other option

5% will never change

In other words, 75% of the change community will probably adopt a 'wait and see' attitude to the change. You may not be able to speed this up no matter what you do!

Therefore, in the early stages of a change program if you are confident you are doing the right things then stick with these things even if initial results are not yet visible.

Principle 11: Expect unexpected change!
You need to be ready to change the change program.

Agility is defined as being able to handle unexpected change well. Nowhere is agility needed more than in leading a change management program and there is nothing more absurd and powerless as a totally rigid change management program!

Strategy & Business Magazine in an article '10 Principles of Change Management [8],' puts it very well:

'*Prepare for the unexpected. No change program goes completely according to plan. People react in unexpected ways; areas of anticipated resistance fall away; and the external environment shifts...Fed by real data from the field and supported by information and solid decision-making processes, change leaders can then make the adjustments necessary to maintain momentum and drive results.*'

A Systematic Introduction to Change Management

Principle 12: Finally, ...rip up that change cookbook...
Sometimes you need to try something creative.

According to the change management experts [7] one of the biggest mistakes you can make in change management is relying too much on activity-based change management programs rather than results-based programs.

Changing peoples' attitudes and behaviors is far from scientific and much too complex a topic to succeed if you rely on standard change management templates and checklists.

So never forget you are dealing with individuals and don't ignore your instincts even if these same instincts are suggesting something rather unconventional is required to break a logjam in the program. But it's a good idea to check your crazy idea out with a thinking partner before jumping in feet first!

A Systematic Introduction to Change Management

Chapter References

1. *The irrational side of change management, The McKinsey Quarterly, 2009.* http://www.mckinsey.com/business-functions/organization/our-insights/the-irrational-side-of-change-management

2. *Leading Change: Why Transformation Efforts Fail,* John P Kotter, Harvard Business School Press, 1996.

3. *In Change Management, Start with Champions, not Antagonists,* Mark Murphy, Forbes Magazine, 2015.

4. *Organizational Change Management Strategies in Modern Business*, edited by Asil Goksoy, IGI Global, 2015.

5. *The Nature of Opposition*, www.changingminds.org. http://changingminds.org/disciplines/change_management/stakeholder_change/nature_opposition.htm

6. *Understanding & Managing Reactions to Change,* Gateshead Council, 2009. https://www.gateshead.gov.uk/DocumentLibrary/council/pois/managingreactionstochange.pdf

7. *Successful Change Programs begin with results*, Robert Schafer and Harvey Thompson, Harvard Business School Press, 1992.

8. *10 Principles of Change Management*, Strategy & Business Magazine, 2004. http://www.strategy-business.com/article/rr00006?gko=643d0

*A Systematic Introduction to
Change Management*

CHANGE MANAGEMENT BASICS

Change Models

There are a number of different metaphors or <u>lenses</u> for change each which can help our thinking as we develop change strategies and plans. Here are 4 of the most useful:

LENS 1: New Habits Model

In this model, we say that the ultimate goal of any change is to have a group of individuals learn a set of new practices which become so deeply ingrained they become new habits. This model helps us focus on what these new habits need to be and also which old habits will need to be 'unlearned'. This allows us to work backward from the New Habits, to the New Behaviors, to the New Practices and to the New Mindsets.

LENS 2: Infection Model

In this model, we think of change as a biological infection or disease. This can help us think of the 'places in the organizational body' which would be most vulnerable to the infection. It can also help us think about different strategies for spreading the infection such as 'word of mouth' or champions. A downside of this model is the negative connotation of an organizational disease. This can be addressed by thinking instead of an 'Antidote' model however you need to be careful that this does not dilute its usefulness as a change thinking tool.

A Systematic Introduction to Change Management

LENS 3: Five Stages of Grief Model

The model was introduced by psychiatrist Elisabeth Kübler-Ross in her book, *On Death and Dying*, and was inspired by studying attitudes of terminally ill patients to their death.

The five stages, popularly known by the acronym DABDA, are:

1. DENIAL
2. ANGER
3. BARGAINING
4. DEPRESSION
5. ACCEPTANCE

The 5 stages in this grief model can be used or suitably adapted for change management – for example:

1. AWARENESS
2. CONSIDERATION
3. EXPERIMENTATION
4. ADOPTION
5. COMMITMENT

Unlike death, however at any of these stages an individual can permanently REJECT the change altogether!

This model can be used to assess what percentage of the target community are at in each stage with respect to the proposed change. It can also very powerfully identify 'The Chasm,' which represents the challenge of getting those individuals who are neither 'Visionaries' nor 'Early Adopters' to embrace the change ('Early Majority', 'Late Majority' and 'Laggards').

A Systematic Introduction to Change Management

Application of the Stages model and development of effective Chasm-Crossing Strategies is explained in detail in Geoffrey Moore's 1998 ground-breaking book 'Crossing the Chasm'.

Appendix 2 describes another model for change from the perspective of running a successful Change Management Project — *The Head, Hearts, Hands & Feet Model*.

LENS 4: The ICE Model (Kurt Lewin)
In Lewin's model, you consider change using the metaphor of an Ice Sculptor who is working on a complex ice statue or palace.

There are 3 stages - *Unfreeze, Change*, and *Freeze*. You start by chunking your proposed change up into a number of phases then you begin.

The Unfreeze stage is then about getting ready for the change.

The Change stage is where the changes are made.

The Freeze stage is where you stabilize what you have achieved and make sure it is well established before you move on. Then you go back to the Unfreeze stage and do it all again for the next phase of the change.

During the Unfreeze stage, you can use a technique which Lewin calls 'Force Field Analysis' to help you consider all the 'forces' which are for and against the change. See the simple example Force Field Analysis overleaf.

Each force can be assigned a score and you then can add up all the scores for each column (for and against). It is important to involve a good broad set of participants in the

A Systematic Introduction to Change Management

force field analysis to ensure that the most important factors are all identified.

Although Lewin's model has been around for some time (the early 1950's) it is still very popular largely because of its powerful simplicity. There are some criticisms, for example, some consider the Freeze stage unworkable for complex change programmes which include multiple changes all to the same deadline.

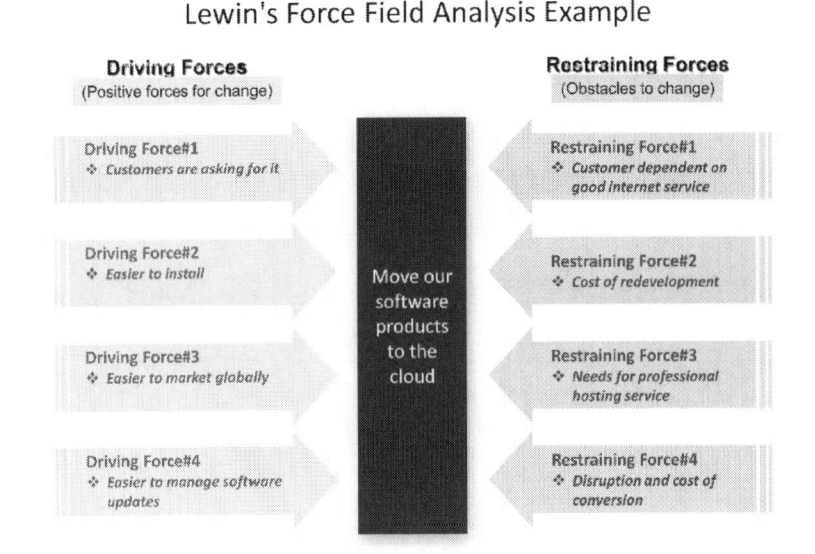

Lewin's Force Field Analysis Example

Driving Forces (Positive forces for change)

- Driving Force#1
  - Customers are asking for it
- Driving Force#2
  - Easier to install
- Driving Force#3
  - Easier to market globally
- Driving Force#4
  - Easier to manage software updates

Move our software products to the cloud

Restraining Forces (Obstacles to change)

- Restraining Force#1
  - Customer dependent on good internet service
- Restraining Force#2
  - Cost of redevelopment
- Restraining Force#3
  - Needs for professional hosting service
- Restraining Force#4
  - Disruption and cost of conversion

Change Models Exercise

What were the underpinning change models in change projects which you have either been involved in or impacted by? *Note these underpinning models may not have been made explicit in the programmes!*

What do you consider to be the biggest single advantage and disadvantage of any change models you have used?

A Systematic Introduction to Change Management

Change Narratives

Now we need to start by creating a compelling change narrative otherwise, we will have no context and no possibility of real engagement. A different chasm metaphor can be helpful here.

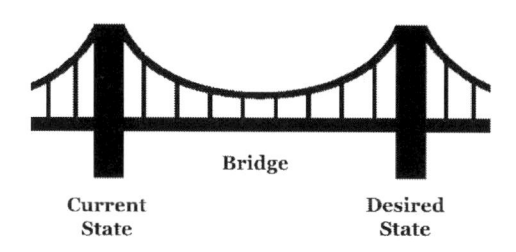

On the one side of the chasm we have the <u>Current State</u>; on the other side of the chasm, we have the <u>Desired State</u>. Between these two we have the <u>Change Project</u> which is the bridge between the two sides.

Let's look at the two sides of the chasm first.

For a change project to have any chance of success one of two situations needs to exist. Either the Current State must be unbearable or the Desired State must be very attractive. The best situation is where both conditions are part of the change story.

Change projects where the Current State is unbearable are often known as 'Burning Platform' projects in contrast to situations where unless there is change a 'Golden Opportunity' will be missed.

It is generally accepted wisdom in the change management community that 'Burning Platform' change stories tend to have more chance of success than 'Golden Opportunity' change stories. One reason for this may be because Safety and Security are more fundamental needs than Esteem and Self-actualization according to *Maslow's Hierarchy of Needs*.

Maslow's Hierarchy of Needs

5- Self-Actualization
4 - Esteem
3 – Love and Belonging
2 - Safety and Security
1 - Physiological

In developing your change narrative or story, you need to think through and 'road test' answers which will stand up to robust challenge by the toughest skeptics in your organization who will question:

- Why do we need to change?
- What is the main reason for the change (Burning Platform or Golden Opportunity or both)?
- Why do we need to change now when we did not need to change before?
- Why can't we defer this change until next year?
- Who decided that we need to change anyway?
- What is the hard measurable evidence for change?
- Do all our leaders believe this change is essential?
- Have we fully examined the consequences of not changing?
- Has anyone else successfully made this change yet?
- What is the *Business Case* for the change (see over)?

A Systematic Introduction to Change Management

Business Cases

Along with the Change Narrative, there should also be a Business Case which estimates the costs and the benefits of the proposed change.

This should really have been produced before the change management plan but if it has not been or it is inadequate you will need to revisit it.

More details on Business Cases plus definitions and examples of the different types of *Return on Investment* calculations are provided in Appendix 1.

Change Narrative Exercise

Review the background material on *TechVet* (a fictitious company) provided in Appendix 3.

Construct an executive summary (1-2 pages) *Change Narrative* for the *TechVet* ERP Project.

You should refer to the principles outlined in this chapter and also the chapter on the Core Principles of Change Management.

A Systematic Introduction to Change Management

Change Planning

This brings us on to the bridge over the chasm – i.e. the Change Project to take us from the Current State to the Desired State. Your colleagues will need to hear convincing answers about the 'how' of change and sceptics will ask hard questions such as:

- Have we a realistic change plan?
- Have we the appetite to see the change through?
- Can we afford the money and resources to do the job properly at this point in time?
- Have we learned from our previous change failures?
- What is the risk we might just make things even worse?

I share with you overleaf a checklist which I call "The 9 Cs of Successful Change Planning."

Each C defines a critical aspect of a change plan in a couple of lines.

Please note that the 9C's does not constitute your actual change plan – it is simply a check whether your change plan is covering all the key areas.

You will still need to develop a realistic change plan which is appropriately detailed for the scale of change envisaged!

A Systematic Introduction to Change Management

Change Planning Checklist

1. Campaign
What is the end result which must be achieved by when?

2. Context:
Why is this project so important now?

3. Community
Who are the key players who are tasked with achieving this result, in other words, the core team?

4. Conclusions
What are the major conclusions (or even better 'transformations') which need to be achieved to deliver the overall results required?

5. Critical Indicators
What are the critical indicators which will give you <u>early warning</u> of problems (*Leading Indicators*) AND <u>ultimate measures</u> of success or failure (*Lagging Indicators*)?

6. Constituencies
Who are the main Constituencies or interest groups who can help or hinder the achievement of the desired end result and how will they be engaged?

7. Constraints
What are the Constraints the change project must work within? These could include resources, money, skills, time or access.

8. Complications
What are the Complications which make the objectives more difficult to achieve than it would appear from the outside looking in? How will they be overcome?

9. Changes
Finally, what are the main Changes or Risks which if they happened would stop the goal being achieved and how will you mitigate against these changes or risks?

A Systematic Introduction to Change Management

Change Planning Exercise

Use the change planning checklist on the previous page to quickly review a change project that you are currently involved with or is impacting you.

Does it highlight any gaps or potential deficiencies or lack of knowledge on your part?

What are you going to do about it?

A Systematic Introduction to Change Management

CHANGE MANAGEMENT TECHNIQUES

3 Principles for Engaging Individuals

Now we have looked at change models, change stories and change planning we need to look at Change Techniques for engaging the key individuals.

From research and practical experience, there are 4 aspects of individual change management which seem fundamental to any change:

1. Insight and Relationship
2. Understanding and Influencing
3. Gaining Commitment
4. Support and Development

These four aspects have an implied sequence 1 -> 2 -> 3 -> 4 to reflect 3 key change management principles namely, that you should:

- *Build rapport and relationship before you have serious conversations with people.*
- *Explore what people feel and want before you ask a person to commit to anything.*
- *Provide support to anyone who has made a commitment to you or is struggling.*

Overleaf, I expand each of these aspects further into 9 specific interventions.

A Systematic Introduction to Change Management

Change Engagement Model

There are 4 key aspects of engaging any individual – these are summarized in the figure below:

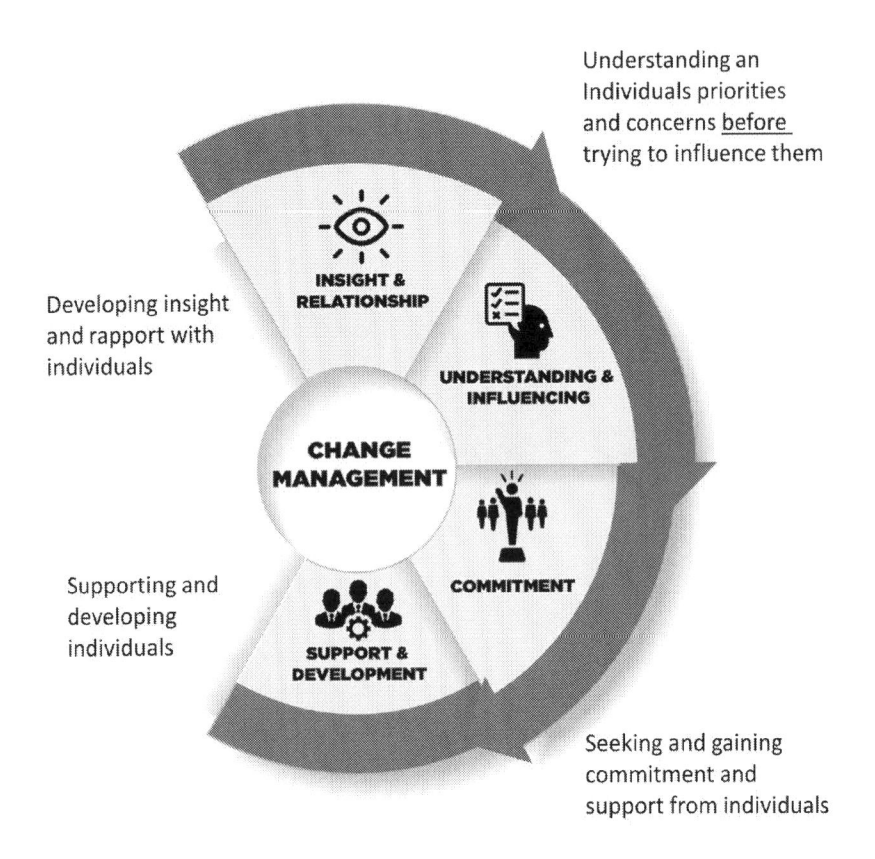

Understanding an Individuals priorities and concerns <u>before</u> trying to influence them

Developing insight and rapport with individuals

INSIGHT & RELATIONSHIP

UNDERSTANDING & INFLUENCING

CHANGE MANAGEMENT

COMMITMENT

Supporting and developing individuals

SUPPORT & DEVELOPMENT

Seeking and gaining commitment and support from individuals

A Systematic Introduction to Change Management

Here are some suggestions, not intended to be exhaustive, on specific interventions you might make in each area:

Insight & Relationships

Here you might consider:

- Gathering information about an individual.
- Meeting with an individual informally.

Understanding & Influencing

Here you might consider:

- Seeking an individual's views or advice about the proposed change.
- Working with an individual to help them deal with the change.
- Seeking feedback from an individual about issues they might have with you, colleagues, or the proposed change.

Commitment

Here you might consider:
- Engaging an individual about their views or advice on the proposed change.
- Asking an individual to support you and become a champion for the change.

A Systematic Introduction to Change Management

Support & Development

Here you might consider:

- Helping and encouraging an individual to play a change champion role.
- Conducting a coaching and development conversation with an individual around change championing.

So what does it mean to be a Change Champion?

In my view there are 3 potential sub-roles involved in being a 'Change Champion':

- *Change Exemplar*s are great examples of colleagues who have adopted the change wholeheartedly and effectively, <u>appropriate to their organizational roles, so</u> that you can point to these people as models of the change working well.
- *Change Advocates* listen to their colleagues and can persuasively argue the case for the change.
- *Change Ambassador*s promote the change in public and group forums within the organization.

When you ask someone to be a 'Change Champion you are asking the person to partner with you in <u>at least one</u> of these sub-roles. You will need to be clear which one (or more) of the sub-roles you wish them to play appropriate to their seniority and influence in the organization. For example, a junior colleague might be great as an operational change exemplar but not so good in front of a crowd as a change ambassador.

A Systematic Introduction to Change Management

Selecting appropriate interventions

There is another very important question you must consider before you start making any interventions with your colleagues:

How do you know which intervention to make with each individual?

There are 3 things you need to determine before you choose specific change management interventions for an individual:

1. **Insight:** How well you know the individual and what is the health of your relationship?
2. **Attitude:** How do they view the proposed change?
3. **Influence:** How influential they are with their colleagues?

Let's look at each of these in a bit more detail:

Insight and Relationship
This is fairly obvious and relates directly to one of the 3 change management principles discussed earlier. If you lack insight or relationship, you should address this before going any further. It is said that there exists a bridge of rapport between any two individuals. If the relationship is weak, then this bridge is like a fragile wooden structure, and if it is strong, it is more like a robust concrete and steel construction. Only one of these bridges will allow 10-ton trucks to drive across it!

Attitude
You can place a person into one of three attitudes with respect to any potential future event, and upcoming

A Systematic Introduction to Change Management

change is no exception. Are they <u>for</u> it, are they <u>against</u> it or are they <u>neither</u> for nor against it!

In other words, are they *Supporters, Opponents* or *Neutrals*?

You need to make sure you don't confuse a relationship issue between an individual and yourself with their attitude to the change. It is possible for a colleague to have a poor relationship with you and be a supporter of the change proposal. Likewise, a colleague you get on with really well could be an opponent of the change proposition!

Charles Spinosa has identified that there is, in fact, a fourth important attitude which is not normally captured in a standard change management Stakeholder Map – 'Ambivalence'. Ambivalence, without closer examination, may appear as either Neutrality or Opposition but this shallow interpretation can be very misleading.

Individuals can be ambivalent due to suspicion, confusion or lack of information, and if this is the case, once the individual's issue has been resolved they may quickly spring to their authentic attitude which could be Support, Neutrality or Opposition.

Influence

Best practice in change management suggests firstly that you should build your change around your *high influence supporters* who can become your *champions* and influence others. Secondly, you should not worry too much initially about *opponents* unless they are *high influence opponents,* who if not carefully engaged with, could turn into *saboteurs* and derail your plans. Finally, *neutrals* will be influenced by the early adopters (and detractors). So, if

A Systematic Introduction to Change Management

you build strong momentum with the right champions, the *neutrals* and remaining *opponents* will be relatively easy to bring on board in due course.

This brings us to the important question of how do you assess an individual's influence with their colleagues?

There are two main types of influence in work situations: organizational influence and social influence.

Organizational influence depends on the person's position in the hierarchy or in a flat structure, their experience or length of service.
Social influence depends on the person's reputation and the extent of their social network in the organization.

So, an individual with a strong reputation and a great social network could be very influential despite the fact that they might be quite junior and not the holder of one of the most senior job titles in the organization. It is important to note that they need a good reputation and a good social network to have social influence. A person with just one of the two could be a *secret guru* (weak network) or a *friendly lightweight* (weak reputation).

You might find the *Colleague Assessment Sheet* overleaf helpful in assessing each of your colleagues. The template helps you systematically assess Their Attitude to The Change, Your Influence on the colleague and Their Influence on others. The first line on the template provides an example of how to complete it for a colleague.

See also the 'Stakeholder Map' discussed in the core principles of Change Chapter.

A Systematic Introduction to Change Management

Now another key question following on from this discussion of organizational and social influence is:

Q: Which is more powerful — organizational influence or social influence?

A: It depends!

In general, in well-established or large organizations organizational influence counts for most, whereas in start-ups, small and non-traditional enterprises social influence can be the most important.

A Systematic Introduction to Change Management

Colleague Assessment Sheet

Summarise positions using High/Medium/Low

COLLEAGUE NAME	THEIR ATTITUDE[1]	YOUR RELATIONSHIP	YOUR INSIGHT ->	YOUR INFLUENCE	EXPERIENCE	REPUTATION	NETWORKS ->	THEIR INFLUENCE
Fred	Neutral	Low	Low	Low	High	Medium	Medium	High

1. What is their Attitude? Are they a SUPPORTER, NEUTRAL or an OPPONENT?

A Systematic Introduction to Change Management

Finally, a very useful technique to help establish the Social Influence of individuals is Social Network Analysis (SNA).

SNA involves constructing a map of the relationships between every member of a group based on analysis of their communication patterns.

You can read more about Social Network Analysis in the next section on Change Management Tools.

Types of Influence Exercise

Which of the two influencing dynamics (*organizational influence or social influence*) carries more weight in your own organization.

How could you use this insight in any change activities you are managing?

*A Systematic Introduction to
Change Management*

CHANGE MANAGEMENT TOOLS

In this section I will review some useful tools to support Change Management:

- Social Network Analysis (SNA)
- Change Risk Assessment (DICE)
- Community Change Visualisation (RIVER Diagram)
- Change Management Simulation (COHORT)
- Change Planning Simulation (SPREAD)

Please note we have already introduced two other important Change Management tools:

- Stakeholder Mapping (Change Principles section)
- Force Field Analysis (Change Models section)

SNA: Social Network Analysis

A very useful technique to help establish the Social Influence of individuals is Social Network Analysis (SNA). SNA involves constructing a map of the relationships between every member of a group based on analysis of their communication patterns.

SNA can be done formally by analysis of email traffic in conjunction with one-to-one interviews with each of the individuals in the group. You need to ask the individuals essentially two questions across two domains – social interactions and work interactions:

- Who do you talk to most socially?
- Who talks to you most socially?
- Who do you go to most for information or help?
- Who comes to you most for information or help?

This information is then used to construct a 'sociogram' which is a two-dimensional matrix summarizing all the interactions among all the individuals. The sociogram can then be analyzed, using freely available or commercial SNA software, to reveal useful information on network roles within the group.

Such a full analysis may be overkill for many change management projects however it is possible to gather most of the necessary information informally and analyze it WITHOUT using more than a spreadsheet. For example, there is an excellent free Microsoft Excel SNA add-in called *NodeXL* — although basic Excel might be all you need!

A Systematic Introduction to Change Management

For example, you could conduct a series of 5-minute interviews by phone or sit down with a few colleagues who know the whole group well and construct a rough sociogram as a team workshop exercise.

Once you have constructed the group sociogram it is possible to analyze the network in many different ways. SNA may initially seem a bit daunting with all its different measures however there are 3 measures which can be very helpful in gaining insight about the connectivity of individuals in your group – Degrees Centrality, Betweenness and Closeness.

Degrees Centrality
Who have the most direct relationships in the network? High centrality tells you a person is well-connected which is good for social influence. However, this measure does not tell you how well the person's connections are connected! They might form a closed group or clique which is not so good for social influence!

Betweenness
This dreadful term directly addresses the reality that often groups are fragmented into 2 or 3 sub-groups which are only weakly connected to each other. A person with high 'Betweenness' can be a bridge between different parts of a network which is good for social influence. However, such a person could also be a bottleneck which is not so good for social influence!

Closeness
Closeness is different from Centrality and Betweenness and measures the individuals who have the best 'access' to the network as a whole taking into account their closeness or proximity to the other network members.

SNA can help you understand 3 key things about a WHOLE GROUP or community:

1. Intrinsic connectivity of the whole group
How well is information flowing around the group as a whole?

2. Inter-departmental connections
How well are the different sub-groups connected to each other?

3. Informal networks
What informal teams exist across departmental boundaries?

SNA can also help you identify 3 key types of INDIVIDUALS in a group:

a. Brokers
Who are the people who act as "glue" between others?

b. Bottlenecks
Who are the people who everybody wants to talk to and are a constraint on overall group productivity?

c. Bystanders
Who are the people who are disconnected from the group?

If you are interested in reading more about SNA there is an excellent two-part introduction to Social Network Analysis written by *Richard Cross* as a guest article on my blog at: http://www.bioteams.com/2006/03/28/social_network_analysis.html

A Systematic Introduction to Change Management

DICE: A Change Risk Assessment Technique

An important article, The Hard Side of Change Management [1] by Hal Sirkin, Perry Keenan and Alan Jackson of the Boston Consulting Group appeared in the October 2005 edition of Harvard Business Review.

Based on assessments of more than 200 major change initiatives, the authors were able to show that the outcome of change initiatives come down to just 4 basic elements - DICE:

1. (D)uration of the project
2. (I)ntegrity of the team
3. Organizational (C)ommitment to change
4. Additional (E)ffort required of staff members

The significance of this is that DICE provides you with a simple and well-evidenced technique to enable you to conduct a risk assessment of a proposed change before you start it. The way it works is that interviews are carried out with executives and leaders of project teams, ideally before they start, and the project DICE score is calculated according to a simple formula with each of the four success indicators being graded on a scale of 1-4 (the lower the score the better).

This score then places a project in one of three zones - a 'Win Zone', a 'Worry Zone' or a 'Woe Zone'. This allows the organization to address key issues or cancel projects altogether if the chance of success is too remote.

How to calculate the DICE Score

There are a number of descriptions of DICE online, perhaps unusually the Wikipedia entry [2] seems to be the only one which summarizes the actual calculation, sourced from another paper [3] which expands the components of DICE as follows:

Duration (D)
either the total duration of short projects or the time between two milestones on longer projects

Team Performance Integrity (I)
the project team's ability to execute successfully, with specific emphasis on the ability of the project leader

Commitment (C)
levels of support, composed of two factors:
C1 visible backing from the sponsor and senior executives for the change
C2 support from those who are impacted by the change

Effort (E)
how much effort will it require to implement (above and beyond business as usual)

The DICE score is calculated according to the following formula:

D + (2 x I) + (2 x C1) + C2 + E

A Systematic Introduction to Change Management

D - Duration
< 2 months = 1
2-4 months = 2
4-8 months = 3
> 8 months = 4

I - Team Performance Integrity
Very good = 1
Good = 2
Average = 3
Poor = 4

C1 - Commitment (Senior Management)
Clearly and strongly communicate the need = 1
Seem to want success = 2
Neutral = 3
Reluctant = 4

C2 - Commitment (Local)
Eager = 1
Willing = 2
Reluctant = 3
Strongly Reluctant = 4

E - Effort
< 10% additional = 1
10-20% additional = 2
20-40% additional = 3
> 40 % additional = 4

Interpreting your DICE Score

A DICE score between 7 and 14 is in the "Win" Zone (very likely to succeed), while a DICE score between 14 and 17

A Systematic Introduction to Change Management

falls in the "Worry" Zone (hard to predict success), and a DICE score higher than 17 falls in the "Woe" Zone (indicating high unpredictability or likely to not succeed).

A simple worked DICE example

Let's imagine an extremely challenging change with all 5 DICE factors scored at 4 to reflect:

- Greater than 8 months' project duration (D)
- Team Performance Integrity is Poor (I)
- Senior Management Commitment is reluctant (C1)
- Local Commitment is strongly reluctant (C2)
- Greater than 40 % additional effort required (E)

Total DICE score is calculated as:

D + (2 x I) + (2 x C1) + C2 + E

which in this case is 28 (4 +8 + 8 + 4 + 4).

This puts the proposed change massively into the Woe Zone (beyond 17) and thus requiring a fundamental rethink about the change to see how the risk could be reduced substantially.

A Systematic Introduction to Change Management

References

1. *The Hard Side of Change Management*, Hal Sirkin, Perry Keenan and Alan Jackson, Harvard Business Review, 2005.
2. *DICE framework*, Wikipedia. https://en.wikipedia.org/wiki/DICE_framework
3. *DICE - How to Beat the Odds in Program Execution*, Perry Keenan and Alan Jackson, The Boston Consulting Group, 2005.

Change Risk Assessment Exercise

Use the DICE Calculation on the previous page to quickly review a change project that you are currently involved with or is impacting you.

Which Risk Zone have you put it in?

Does it highlight any gaps or potential deficiencies or lack of knowledge on your part?

What are you going to do about it?

A Systematic Introduction to Change Management

RIVER DIAGRAM: Community Change Visualisation

The River Diagram is a neat strategic visualization tool for helping to move a 'community of groups' forward via common initiatives and best practice sharing. I am grateful for Chris Collison who introduced me to it.

The River Diagram is useful if you have a number of groups or constituencies who are all working independently but on the same set of common challenges.

It helps you see instantly where the common issues are and where experience could be shared, supported by the common language from a maturity model or self-assessment framework, ideally one which was co-created by the participants

The example fragment of a River Diagram overleaf is taken from an Evaluation of the UNAIDS/UNITAR AIDS Competence Programme [1].

On the x-axis, you plot the different behaviors to be addressed and on the y-axis, you record a score for each behavior on a scale 1-5. In other words, you start with a Maturity Model for each key element of the particular Change you are working on.

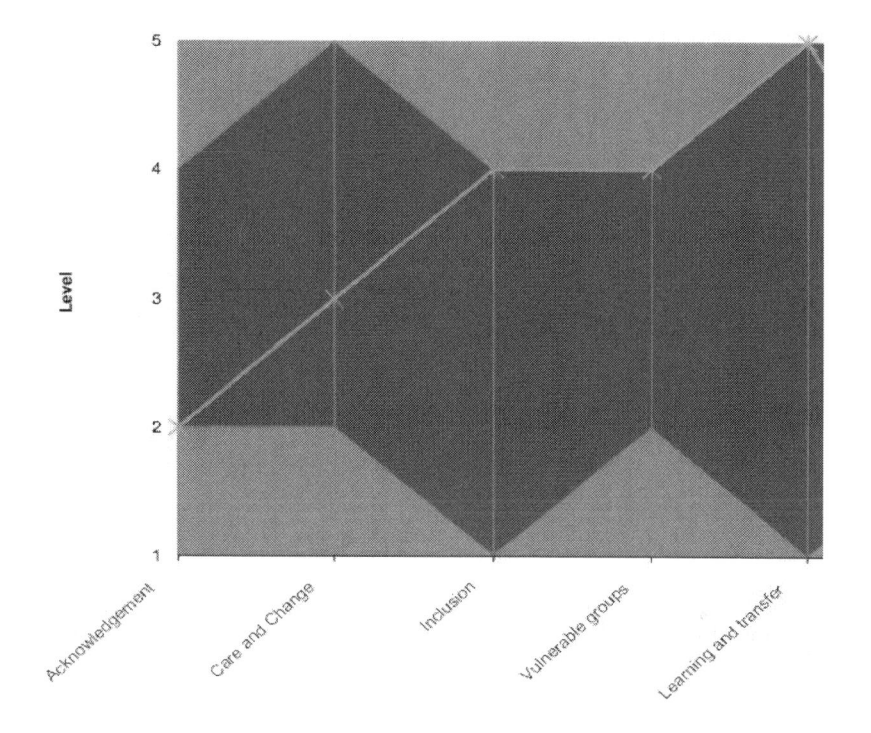

A Systematic Introduction to Change Management

[Chart showing Level (1-5) on y-axis with categories on x-axis: Acknowledgement, Care and Change, Inclusion, Vulnerable groups, Learning and transfer]

First, you assess each group individually across each of the behaviors. The south bank of the river is the lowest maturity score for any of the groups for each behavior and the north bank of the river is the highest maturity score for the groups.

Therefore, in the example, on the extreme left of the diagram data point, 1 is "Awareness of HIV/AIDs". This shows that all groups have achieved at least Level 1 (South Bank), the remaining groups are between Level 2 and Level 4 (the River) and no group has yet achieved Level 5 (North Bank). The pink line represents the scores from one of the communities which used the maturity tool, and shows their score relative to the spread of all other scores as a backdrop (the River).

A Systematic Introduction to Change Management

The River Diagram reveals 3 things:

1. The South Bank – Issues addressed by all
This reflects how much the groups as a whole have already achieved - this is the current community baseline. Every group has at least reached here.

2. The North Bank – Issues remaining for all
This reflects the elements none of the groups have yet been able to address. Here is the best place for initiatives for all the groups. You would need to decide, from the context, whether these initiatives could be rolled out at the same time to all groups or whether they would need to be piloted with specific groups first.

3.The River – The Best can help the Worst
This shows you the leaders and laggers for each of the behaviors and therefore highlights the opportunities for the leaders to help the laggers move their performance towards the North Bank. The amount each lagger can move depends on their appetite - they can't all move to the North Bank in one move!

I asked Chris about his experience of what the River Diagram can really offer in practice:

"Everyone has something to learn, and everyone has something to share. The shape of the river shows the potential for sharing knowledge and learning within the group. In a learning organization, it should change over time, gradually 'eroding the north bank, and laying up sediment on the south bank', as some groups innovate new practices and others lift themselves up from the basics of level 1."

References

1. Evaluation of the UNAIDS/UNITAR AIDS Competence Programme, Unitar, 2005 (especially page 74). http://data.unaids.org/Publications/IRC-pub06/jc1144-evaluation-unitar_en.pdf

A Systematic Introduction to Change Management

COHORT: Change Simulation Game

COHORT is a computer-based business simulation game designed specifically to illustrate the concepts discussed in this guide.

Specifically, the simulation allows leaders and managers, playing teams against their colleagues, to practice their change management influencing skills in a safe environment.

At the start of the simulation, the participants analyze briefing material on the target organization which can either be totally fictitious or similar to their own organization.

A Systematic Introduction to Change Management

Briefing materials, in the forms of bios, are also provided for each of ten directors in the organization. There are two types of bios – public bios (which are freely available to everyone) and private bios (which are only discovered after you begin to engage with a specific individual).

There is also an organization chart which indicates the organizational influence and a social network which represents the social influence in terms of the relationships, reputations and social interactions at work.

The simulation uses agent-based simulation techniques so that any time you influence any individual this also has some effect on all the other individuals depending on that individual's organizational and social influence.

The briefing materials provide the necessary information to determine the required change management intervention per individual, team or whole group.

The simulation uses the latest experiential and social learning techniques to amplify the learning. Simulations typically run for half a day with 3-4 teams each of 4-6 players.

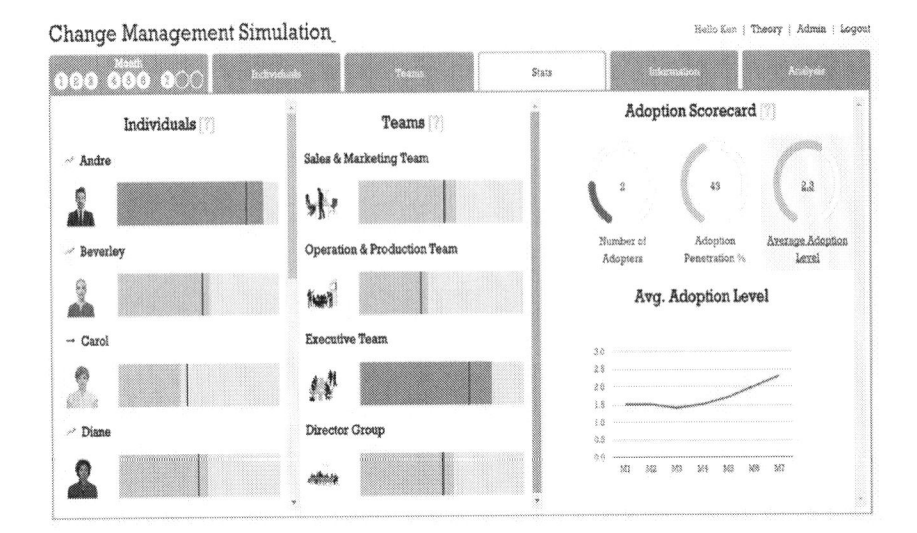

A Systematic Introduction to Change Management

Developing your teams and leadership styles

A team-based simulation, such as COHORT, can be used not just develop understanding of change management but also to learn about team dynamics and individual leadership styles.

For more details, please see 'Appendix 4: High Performing Teams in a hurry!'

You can find out more about COHORT here: http://dashboardsimulations.com/business-games/cohort-change-management/

A Systematic Introduction to Change Management

SPREAD: Community Change Simulation

Spread is a computer-based business simulation which provides a 'what-if' planning capability for any change which involves rolling out a new practice or innovation to a well-defined community using *one-many* interventions.

Specifically, the simulation allows leaders and managers, to explore the effectiveness and sequencing of different types of one-many interventions to attempt to move a whole community from 'unaware' to 'fully adopted'.

In technical terms, Spread is a Change Diffusion Model.

Spread can be customized for the organization, change and target community, and therefore can be used as a management tool to 'test and tune' the planning of a mass change. For example, Spread has been used in healthcare to model the roll-out of new healthcare practices ('the innovation') within defined practitioner groups ('the target community').

Spread can be played as a team game to educate players about the change and to develop wider ownership for the change across a change leadership team.

Typical Spread uses include New Product Launch within external customer communities or New Strategy / Process / Behavior Roll-out within internal organizational communities.

After a group has played Spread to prepare for an upcoming major change rollout they should understand much more clearly what is really involved.

A Systematic Introduction to Change Management

Therefore, they should be better equipped to envisage it, plan it, identify the key risks and manage more effectively when the unexpected happens because they have already simulated it!

Spread can be configured with any set of tasks required for a rollout and all team decisions are saved and can be "action-replayed" afterwards to deepen the learning. Spread results are shown graphically using high impact charts showing user adoption, budget spend, user benefits and other key roll-out measures.

The diagram below summarises the different type of initiatives which can be applied to a community change with Spread.

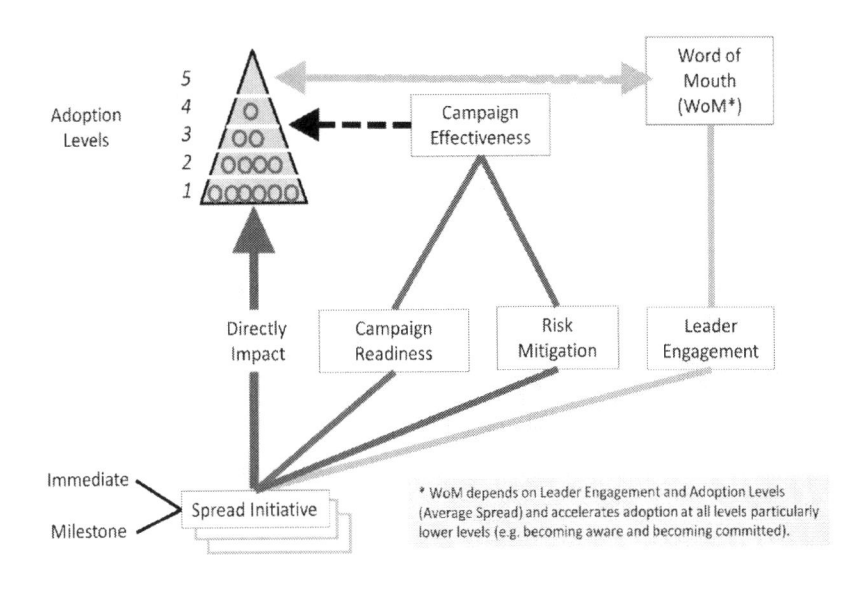

* WoM depends on Leader Engagement and Adoption Levels (Average Spread) and accelerates adoption at all levels particularly lower levels (e.g. becoming aware and becoming committed).

A Systematic Introduction to Change Management

Below is a screenshot from a typical Spread session. On the left we have a list of possible spread initiatives and their status. The 4 gauges show graphically the progress on Readiness, Leader Engagement, Milestones and Adoption.

The charts and the table to the right show how user adoption is moving through the different stages from Unaware right through to Sustaining.

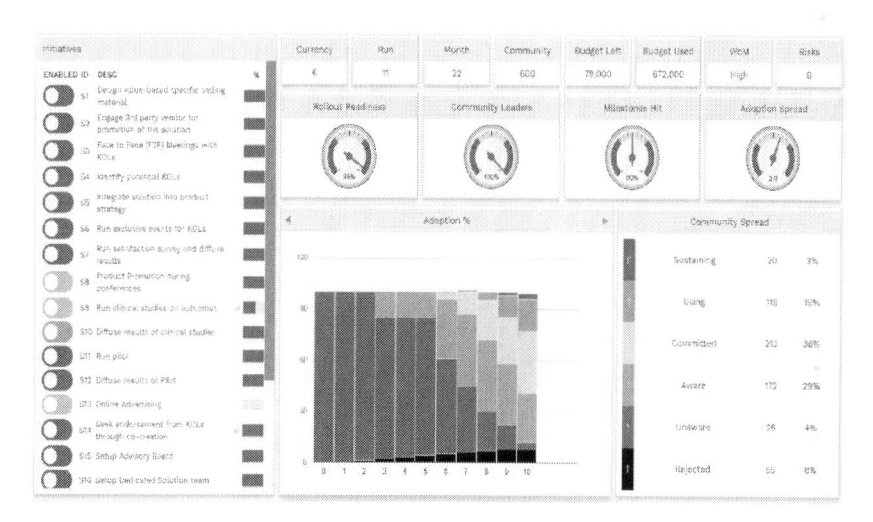

Spread can be configured for any number of initiatives which might be required for the specific roll-out programme and can include:

- Once-off Initiatives or Repeatable a maximum number of times
- Require single or multiple periods to complete (Milestones)
- Initiatives which depend on other activities completing before they can commence
- Initiatives which can be repeated but with a time delay between them

A Systematic Introduction to Change Management

Each Spread Initiative can have any or all off the following characteristics:

- It enhances the readiness of the Rollout Campaign and the effectiveness of all subsequent initiatives
- It engages the Community Leaders to promote 'Word of Mouth viral adoption
- It mitigates against future risks to the rollout
- It directly enables users to move up a level of adoption on a 5-point adoption scale

You can find out more about Spread here: http://dashboardsimulations.com/business-games/spread-innovation-spreader/

A Systematic Introduction to Change Management

INFLUENCING COMMUNITIES: LEADING LARGE-SCALE CHANGE IN THE DIGITAL ERA

Setting the scene

Leading change by influencing senior stakeholders or colleagues or team members is a critically important aspect of change management. However, often this simply creates good foundations for the bigger change story to come.

For change to make a real impact it usually needs to go beyond senior leaders and extend into the bigger front-line communities who these leaders are responsible for or serve as suppliers.

There are countless examples of large-scale change ranging from political campaigns, huge change programmes in public and private organisations and the introduction of new products and services into consumer and company markets.

These changes should all have started with small groups of leaders, focus groups, consumer groups, market researchers, early adopters and internal guinea pigs. That, however was only the appetiser for the main course to come.

In moving from small group change to large-scale community change we will encounter many new challenges such as:

*A Systematic Introduction to
Change Management*

- Engaging with people many of whom we barely know at best
- The impracticality of face-to-face and one-one interactions
- The reliance on virtual and one-many interactions
- The positive and negative aspects of using social media (external and in-company)
- The importance of key influencers in these communities in helping or hindering our change

To be successful in large-scale community change we also need to understand some important points:

- The difference between a community and a crowd - and why it matters
- The role of super-connectors in mass change
- Key types of activity you need in your change campaign
- The risks of email and social media in mass change
- Best Practices in individual and mass persuasion
- Tips for successfully managing large-scale community change

I will now explore each of these topics in more detail.

A Systematic Introduction to Change Management

The difference between a community and a crowd - and why it matters

So, what is the difference?

You might say that a community has a shared interest or purpose, but a crowd does not. However, a crowd of football supporters have a shared interest and yet they are still a crowd. So shared interest is necessary but not sufficient to being a community.

You might then say that a community is of a scale which permits regular interaction between most of its members, but a crowd does not. There is something in that, but it is also possible to be part of a very small crowd which is even smaller than some communities. So frequent member interaction is also necessary but not sufficient to being a community.

A good way to appreciate the difference between a community and a small crowd is to think of the difference between a Sports Team and a Fitness Club.

People attend a fitness club to use the exercise equipment and incidentally meet other members. The primary glue is the shared access to expensive equipment and facilities. Meeting other users is not an essential part of the experience. However, people join a Sports Team to play team sports and meeting other players is an essential part of that experience.

The thing which makes a community different from a crowd, in my opinion, is that in a community there is a deep network of relationships spanning the whole community whereas in a crowd there are lots of little

89

localised clusters of relationships. Whilst there may be links between the different clusters in a crowd there is nothing like the extent of cross-network relationships which there are in a community. This topic is explored in the discipline of Social Network Analysis and is discussed in more detail earlier in this guide.

Another way to understand the difference is to say that a community is a "Peer Network" but a crowd is a "Star Network". In a community there is a horizontal network of relationships between peers whereas in a crowd there are small number of "stars" and each member relates to these stars (vertically) much more than they relate to each other (their peers).

Why does this matter for large-scale change management?

The main thing is that it is much easier to engage a community than a crowd. This is because a crowd is really a collection of discrete small groups (clusters) and if you communicate with one of these clusters there is no guarantee that they will pass on your communications to anyone else because they may be only loosely connected to these other clusters. However, in a community the wide network of relationships makes it much easier to propagate any message.

Does this mean you cannot bring change to a crowd? No, of course not. It just means it will be more difficult and you will need to work harder. You really need to think of a crowd as segmented into many mini-communities which are only very loosely linked. To engage such a crowd, you need to engage with each of these mini-communities separately which adds up to much more effort than if it was just one community.

A Systematic Introduction to Change Management

The role of super-connectors in mass change

A key aspect of engaging effectively with a community is to try and identify the key people in the network who have a) the most relationships and b) best authority and try to collaborate with them to pass on your messages. Let's call them "super-connectors" but they can also be referred to as community leaders, key influencers and opinion leaders.

There are two types of authority – organizational authority (positional) and social authority (reputational) which are discussed in more detail earlier in this guide. We will focus our discussion here on reputation however the approach can be adapted to communities where organizational authority dominates.

It is important to remember that super-connectors should have both a good network and a good reputation. If they have a good network and a poor reputation they will just be annoying noise generators within the community. On the other hand, if they have a great reputation (perhaps for their expertise in some topic) but are badly connected they may be little use. However, one important caveat applies. If your change message is opposed or discredited by an expert with a small network, it is quite likely that their opinion will get picked up and transmitted by other community members with much bigger networks and your change initiative may have a credibility problem.

Albert-László Barabási, a former Professor at the University of Notre Dame, has researched extensively into the concept of what he calls "scale-free networks" in natural, technological and social systems, from the cellular telephone to the World Wide Web and online communities.

A Systematic Introduction to Change Management

Barbasi has written an excellent book on the subject – "Linked: The New Science of Networks" [1] in which he defines a "scale-free network" as a network whose degree distribution follows a power law. In layman's terms, what this means is that a small percentage of the nodes in such networks have significantly higher connectivity than the other nodes. Barbasi explains how the scale-free network structure applies to human networks which have "super-connectors" who have much higher levels of connectivity than anyone else in the network.

A key element of promoting change in a community is identifying and collaborating with these super-connectors to spread the change through the community. It is interesting to note that you can also have super-connectors within a crowd but to a much lesser degree.

Working with super-connectors is a double-edged sword. They can be difficult, arrogant and impetuous. They can oppose you. They can turn from supporters into opponents overnight. They can make your life very difficult. They can have a huge sense of their own importance. They may be hugely demanding of your time and attention. They can delay you with suggested changes to your approach.

However super-connectors are a fact of community change and without them your change will fail. Super-connectors can create a "word of mouth" dynamic within the community where everyone is talking about your change.

Its entirely up to you whether they are saying good things or bad things about it!

A Systematic Introduction to Change Management

Key types of activity you need in your change campaign

From my experience [2], to effectively engage a community you need to consider at least 4 different types of activity:

- Preparedness Activity
- Community Influencer Activity
- Risk Mitigation Activity
- User Adoption Activity

These four types of activity are not mutually exclusive. For example, a specific preparedness activity might also mitigate against an important campaign risk.

Preparedness Activity

This kind of activity is normally conducted before a campaign commences and its purpose is to lay important foundations which will make future engagement activities more effective. Typical examples include setting up steering groups or customer representative panels and developing appropriate written and multimedia assets to support the engagement.

Think of Preparedness Activity as the "Railway Tracks" of your Community Change Campaign.

Community Influencer Activity

Most communities have key individuals who are very influential (see our previous discussion on what defines a community and super-connectors). They can use this influence for or against your community change campaign.

A Systematic Introduction to Change Management

They can also choose to ignore your campaign which will also make it more difficult for you. The first stage is to identify these people within the community. It may be that some of them are very visible and obvious and by engaging with them carefully you may also build up a profile of the characteristics and meeting places of the other ones.

Normally the next stage is to try and get these influencers into an early co-invention conversation about the change to seek their support. You want to see if they are positive and will help you. Alternatively, if they are luke-warm, neutral or opposing you need to listen to their advice and find a way to re-engage them later.

Think of Community Influencer Activity as the "Train Drivers" of your Community Change Campaign.

Risk Mitigation Activity

Strictly speaking risk mitigation activities are special cases of preparedness or community influencer activities. However, they are so important and so frequently missing from community change campaigns that I prefer to treat them as distinct.

When you are planning your campaign, you need to include a risk analysis of what might go wrong. There are two risk perspectives – risks within your control and risks which are outside of your control. Failing to engage certain high-profile influencers would be an example of a risk within your control. Finding yourself in competition with a similar or competing rollout within the same community might be an example of a risk outside of your control.

A Systematic Introduction to Change Management

Both these risks are entirely foreseeable and specific avoidance and mitigation activities can be planned to a) reduce the risk of them happening and/or b) to allow you to respond effectively and quickly if they do occur.

There are other types of risk such as your company being acquired or the government falling which might be much more difficult to foresee. In this case whilst it may not be possible to identify specific mitigations in advance you can still structure your change project in a way that might make them less impactful. For example, by building in contingency time or budget or resources which you do not plan to use if things go well.

A vital risk mitigation activity is to build the necessary early warning systems to alert you early if a risk starts materializing. Such systems are typically reporting mechanisms built around the leading indicators of success you will have identified as part of your plan for measuring the success of the project through a Balanced Scorecard approach [3].

Think of Risk Mitigation Activity as the "Signalling System" of your Community Change Campaign.

User Adoption Activity

This final type of activity may represent the bulk of your efforts and time in a community change programme. These are the activities which directly move individuals in the community from one level of adoption to the next.

A useful tool in developing adoption activities is the AIDCA model [4] which is similar to the change adoption model described earlier in this guide but more suited to community engagement and summarised in the table below working from the bottom up:

ACTION	Gaining commitment to the action you want the people to take
CONVICTION	Providing convincing evidence of your idea
DESIRE	Connecting your idea with a person's personal needs and wants
INTEREST	Gaining a person's interest in your idea based on relevance
ATTENTION	Grabbing a person's attention for your idea

To be able to monitor your success you will also need an "Adoption Model" plus some mechanism for identifying when individuals move upwards (or backwards) based on some observable behaviours which you can then build reporting systems around.

For example, the Spread Simulation (described in the previous section) uses a 5-point Adoption Model shown overleaf.

In addition, at any level (1-4) below "Sustaining" on the model a potential user can REJECT (returning to level 0) the change altogether thus becoming closed to any further engagement on the topic.

A crucial element of user adoption activity is to create systems which allow you to track, not just the adoption but, the costs and, where possible, the benefits of any change campaign. The costs are usually easy to track as they are driven by the activities. The benefits are usually related to the adoption levels and can be harder to track and may also extend well beyond the life of the change campaign.

A Systematic Introduction to Change Management

ADOPTION LEVEL	ADOPTION CHARACTERISTICS
SUSTAINING (5)	Embracing the change on an on-going basis and prepared to champion the change to others
USING (4)	Embracing the change on a trial basis but not yet a sustaining habit or practice
COMMITTED (3)	Committed to the change in principle but not yet embracing it
AWARE (2)	Aware of the proposed change but have not yet formed a solid opinion on its worth
UNAWARE (1)	Not aware of the proposed change

Think of User Adoption Activity as the "Ticket Sales" of your Community Change Campaign.

☐

Risks of email and social media in mass change

In large scale community engagement, it is inevitable that much of your user adoption activities will involve email and other forms of electronic communications. In addition, many of these will also be of a one-many nature rather than more personal one-one communications.

These two facts create certain risks including:

- "Mailshot syndrome" where the messages attract a very low response (both open rates and action rates)
- Getting caught in SPAM filters
- Getting lost in the sheer volume of messaging traffic
- Negative reactions if your messages appear to be unsolicited
- Negative feedback loops especially if using social media
- Tendency to over-estimate levels of user engagement achieved

There are 3 specific principles you can apply to help you minimise these risks:

#1 Respect Data Protection and Personal Privacy

You need a person's express permission to email them – you cannot just email somebody whose details you found on a list. Data Protection legislation is becoming tighter year after year with huge fines now for companies who flout the rules [5]. Key areas to look out for include suppression list management where it is your responsibility to maintain and manage accurate lists of both people who have agreed to be mailed on a topic and those who have asked not to be mailed. It is also becoming increasing important that people actively opt-in to receiving your emails as opposed to the older system of them having to opt-out if they do not wish to be mailed. In addition, permission is granted only on a specific topic – just because you previously emailed someone about topic X does not allow you to email them about topic Y unless X and Y can be shown to be are clearly linked.

#2 Normal social etiquette rules still apply digitally

Sometimes when we communicate via electronic messaging we try to get to the point too quickly and in so doing we violate the normal rules of rapport building and social etiquette. It is nearly always better to take an extra email or message to build social rapport before we push for some form of commitment.

#3 Blend the digital and the personal

Research [6] shows that purely digital engagement does not build anything like the levels of rapport you can build face to face. Therefore, make sure that you have built as much physical interaction into your campaign as possible. Examples include lunch-time briefings with small groups, large group presentations and presentation/attendance at relevant conferences targeted at the community. Where you do not have the time or capacity for physical meetings you can always build in telephone calls which although not as good as physical are still much more engaging than any form of email or messaging.

Best practices in individual and mass persuasion

Over the ten years techniques best practices for persuading individuals and groups (communities and crowds) have evolved significantly. Individual Persuasion techniques have developed significantly within business management disciplines. Mass persuasion techniques have developed hugely in advertising and politics. Some of the mass techniques are targeted at large external crowds such as advertising and political campaigning. Your change communities will probably be much smaller than these and quite often your community will be internal to your organisation.

If you are unware of these best practices in individual and group persuasion, then you will probably make some mistakes in your community change campaigns that you do not need to make. To be successful in leading change, whether it is on a one-one basis or in a community or a crowd, you need to be aware of best practices in persuasion including:

- Principled Negotiation
- Influence
- Presuasion
- Behavioural Economics
- Cognitive Dissonance
- Herd Behaviour

I won't attempt a comprehensive review of best practices but instead simply offer a cursory synopsis plus sign-posting of relevant sources where, if you want to, you can study the subjects in more detail.

A Systematic Introduction to Change Management

Principled Negotiation

A critical discipline to master to be successful in leading change is negotiation. As the saying goes "You don't get what you deserve you get what you negotiate." One of most successful approaches to negotiation is known as principle-based or principled negotiation made popular by the book "Getting to Yes" by Roger Fisher and William Ury [7].

Principled negotiation stands in stark contrast to the earlier style of "combative negotiations" where the objective was to emerge as "the winner" of the negotiations. The theory of principled negotiation is that both parties need to be winners otherwise the deal will be sour, not sustainable and consequently poison or even destroy the relationship between the parties.

Fisher and Ury suggest an approach to negotiating which is based around 4 simple principles:

1. Separating the people from the problem
2. Focusing on interests rather than positions
3. Generate options for mutual gain
4. Insist on using objective criteria

Understanding the difference between a position and an interest is central to this approach and is best illustrated by a short story. A husband and wife both want an orange, but they only have one between them. If they negotiate by positions they will split the orange in two. However, if the couple negotiate by interests they may discover that the woman wants the orange peel to make jam and the man wants to eat the orange fruit and can create a "win-win". Note that in negotiation by positions you often end up in a compromise which suits neither party.

A Systematic Introduction to Change Management

Persuasion …. and Presuasion

"Influence: The Psychology of Persuasion" [8] by Robert Cialdini became an instant bestseller when published in 2007 and was hailed by some as the most important book written for marketing in a decade.

Cialdini identifies 7 key influencers of persuasion based on 35 years of applied research:

1. **Weapons of influence** - the reason behind the request
2. **Reciprocation** – creating social obligation (e.g. through generosity) which creates a pressure to reciprocate
3. **Commitment & Consistency** – gaining a commitment, often small, to which the giver may feel obliged to remain consistent
4. **Social Proof** – showing that other people you respect have committed to the topic of the persuasion
5. **Liking** – creating a shared bond with the person you are persuading
6. **Authority** – enhancing your perceived status before you attempt to persuade
7. **Scarcity** – we are usually more motivated by the thought of losing out on something than gaining something

In 2017 Cialdini went on to publish a second and equally successful book "Pre-Suasion: A Revolutionary Way to Influence and Persuade" [9] which addresses the important, but largely unexplored, area of how to get people's attention and to put them in the optimum state for any subsequent persuasion to succeed.

A Systematic Introduction to Change Management

Cialdini suggested that before we start persuading we should try to capture the listener's attention by creating positive associations through imagery and words with the topic of our persuasion. For example, if you want people or groups to try an untested product or service, you should first ask them if they consider themselves to be adventurous. Alternatively, if you want people or groups to be more achievement oriented then you could first provide them with an image of an athlete or team winning a race.

A Systematic Introduction to Change Management

Behavioural Economics

Behavioural Economics (BE) is the discipline of explaining why we do what we do. BE attempts to explain why we are so frequently "predictably irrational" in our decision-making and it identifies many traps, known in BE as biases, which we frequently fall into as individuals or groups.

BE explains why we are systemically and predictably irrational in our economic decisions, and introduces 2 terms "Bounded Rationality" and "Bounded Willpower," as the limits to rationality within which we all operate.

A short synopsis of some of the key biases in BE include:

- Endowment Effect: tendency to place more value on expected losses than expected gains (also known as Risk Aversion)
- Status Quo Bias: tendency to stick with the current position even though we can see clearly better alternatives
- Framing Bias: tendency to draw conclusions according to the way something seems as opposed to reality
- Availability Bias: tendency to rely on easily available information rather than seeking out harder to obtain but more accurate/relevant info
- Confirmation Bias: tendency to prioritize evidence which accords with our pre-existing beliefs
- Choice Overload: where we have so many options we don't make any decision
- Overconfidence Bias: tendency to rate ourselves more knowledgeable and skilful than we are
- Money Illusion: tendency to judge prices and interest rates at nominal rates rather than considering inflation

A Systematic Introduction to Change Management

These biases highlight a key point in persuasion – providing a factual rationale argument is unlikely to be effective when people's biases have been emotionally triggered.

You can read an excellent introduction to BE here [10].

A Systematic Introduction to Change Management

Cognitive Psychology

A fascinating psychological trait known as Cognitive Dissonance can also have a big impact on making it difficult to use facts to persuade people in certain circumstances. You can read a good introduction to Cognitive Dissonance here [11] where the authors suggest:

"Cognitive dissonance refers to a situation involving conflicting attitudes, beliefs or behaviors. This produces a feeling of discomfort leading to an alteration in one of the attitudes, beliefs or behaviors to reduce the discomfort and restore balance, etc. For example, when people smoke (behavior) and they know that smoking causes cancer (cognition)".

Cognitive Dissonance explains why smokers tend to believe that there is a lower connection between cancer and smoking than non-smokers. There is a conflict between the behaviour of smoking and the knowledge that smoking is bad for their health. This is often resolved not by changing the behaviour but by changing the belief.

Cognitive Dissonance also explains why it can be so difficult to get people to change deeply ingrained habits, where the alternative looks so much better to you, by appealing only to their rationality and reason. When we combine the effects of Cognitive Dissonance with BE biases such as the Confirmation Bias we can easily convince ourselves of almost anything we want to believe and then constantly find confirming evidence to justify our positions!

A Systematic Introduction to Change Management

Herd Behaviour

Mark Earls in his book, "Herd: How to change mass behaviour by harnessing our true nature" [12], suggests that persuasion is much less about individual choice/free will and much more about our natural human tendencies to go with the crowd and copy others.

Earls argues:

"This is why most government initiatives struggle to create real change, why so much marketing money fails to drive sales, why M&A programmes actually reduce shareholder value, and most internal change projects don't deliver any lasting transformation."

Earls develops 7 principles of "Herd-based marketing":

1. INTERACTION – mass behaviour results from interactions between individuals in a specific content
2. INFLUENCE – influence not persuasion is the key to shaping mass behavior
3. US-TALK - Word of Mouth is very powerful but can be negative as well as positive
4. JUST BELIEVE – you need to be "interesting" and stand for something
5. LIGHT THE FIRE – focus on overcoming cynicism, lack of purpose and belief
6. CO-CREATIVITY – learn how to work with your communities not simply talk at them
7. LETTING GO – abandon your ideas of certainty and your need to control your communities

A Systematic Introduction to Change Management

He writes:

"Mass behaviour in the urinals, in the lecture theatre, in public spaces, in cars and in football stadiums – is strictly speaking a complex phenomenon. That is, it is the result of individuals interacting with each other and is as such understandable through modelling their rule-based interaction.

The teenagers on the canal side in Camden are gathered there, all dressed the same because others are. The BMW drivers all think they are individuals because they interact most often with people who don't drive BMWs – vanilla car owners as they see them – and respond to the cues of individuality BMW designers and marketers have highlighted."

A Systematic Introduction to Change Management

Tips for successfully managing large-scale community change

Here are some practical tips for managing your community change successfully:

Plan-Do-Check-Act

Like all good projects you should structure your activities round a modern best practice project planning and management approach like the PDCA Cycle [13].

Pilot before Production

A community change project can be one of the most difficult types of project to plan fully in advance. Therefore, I would recommend a pilot-based approach where you first conduct a small pilot project to enable you to make your mistakes small to avoid making them large. I remember only too well the sinking feeling after I sent out my lovely new email newsletter to 1000 of my blog readers with a typo in the title.

Community Segmentation

With the benefit of the learning from your pilot approach you can now start to engage with the wider community. An excellent risk reduction strategy at this point is to segment your target community to try to locate a "small and friendly" subset. You can then engage with this mini community first. If you have selected well, these individuals will tolerate some sub-optimal moves. They will also give you important feedback which will allow you to adjust things before engaging the bigger, less forgiving, community.

A Systematic Introduction to Change Management

Perturbation Management

Once you are into your User Adoption Activities my experience is that you often move to a special form of Change Management which I call Perturbation Management [14]. This is a form of change management where you introduce stimuli and carefully monitor the results. If the results are moving in the right direction you can broaden and intensify the stimulus. If they are not moving or not moving in a helpful direction, then you can try an alternative stimulus perhaps returning to the previous stimulus later.

Simulation

The use of simulation tools, such as Spread [15], outlined in the previous section, allow you to manage different scenarios and risks as you rollout your change in a safe virtual environment. You can also "what-if" different stimuli and sequences of change.

Simulation can be very useful in helping a team envision, plan and execute a community change programme and become better equipped to deal with the unexpected when it arises during the actual rollout.

A Systematic Introduction to Change Management

Chapter References & Further Reading

1. Linked: The New Science of Networks, Albert-László Barabási, Perseus, 2002
2. The Networked Enterprise: Competing for the Future Through Virtual Enterprise Networks, Ken Thompson, MK Press, 2008
3. The Balanced Scorecard: Translating Strategy into Action, Robert Kaplan and David Norton, Harvard, 1996
4. AIDA: Attention-Interest-Desire-Action, Mindtools.com
5. A Summary of the EU General Data Protection Regulation, Peter Galdies, DataIQ, 2017
6. Freeriding in teams, communities and networks: 5 tips for fighting it, Ken Thompson, bioteams.com, 2007
7. Getting to Yes: Negotiating an agreement without giving in, Roger Fisher and William Ury, Random House, 2012
8. Influence: The Psychology of Persuasion, Robert Cialdini, Harper Business, 2007
9. Pre-Suasion: A Revolutionary Way to Influence and Persuade, Robert Cialdini, Random House, 2017
10. An Introduction to Behavioral Economics, Alain Samson, behavioraleconomics.com, 2014
11. Cognitive Dissonance, Saul McLeod, simplypsychology.org, 2008
12. Herd: How to change mass behaviour by harnessing our true nature, Mark Earls, Wiley, 2007
13. Plan-Do-Check-Act (PDCA), Mindtools.com
14. Bioteams: High Performance Teams Based on Nature's Most Successful Designs Paperback, Ken Thompson, MK Press, 2008
15. SPREAD: Innovation Rollout and Large-Scale Change Simulation, dashboardsimulations.com, 2017

A Systematic Introduction to
Change Management

CHANGE MANAGEMENT CASE STUDIES

In this chapter I have pulled together 5 programmes which are considered, sometimes retrospectively, to be examples of major change management programs.

The projects span the international, national and company levels. Some are considered successes, some are viewed as failures and some are in the 'debatable' category.

The 5 projects are:

- Y2K (The Millennium Bug)

- The Good Friday Agreement (The N. Ireland Peace Process)

- Smoking in Public Places

- JC Penney

- Ford Motor Company

The projects are summarized and presented to the reader as exercises to check their understanding of the key principles of change management. My own perspective on each project is also included (at the end).

Finally, I identify a list of other well-known change management projects with references for the reader to study further.

A Systematic Introduction to Change Management

Y2K (The Millennium Bug)

The Challenge:

Coming up to the year 2000 it was realized that software programmers believed it was not a leap year when in fact it was. The rule is a leap year must be divisible by 4 except if it is divisible by 100 but not if it is divisible by 400. There was widespread panic, fuelled by some technology authors who should have known better, about what would happen to computers on 1 January 2000. People were worried about not being able to get money from banks or flying around the date in case their planes fell out of the sky.

Organizations were already under pressure with new strategies, new competitors, acquisitions, plans and other challenges and did not want to hear that they would have to pay to have every single line of code in every single software program checked and potentially fixed. In addition, all new software projects would have to be shelved or take second priority to Y2K work during 1999.

The Results:

There were no publicized software failures arising from Y2K as almost all organizations had invested billions in huge checking and conversion programs starting from as early as 1997. On one hand, it could be argued that it was a storm in a teacup, fully exploited by the IT industry who had, of course, been the original authors of it. On the other hand, no-one was injured or died in a world running a huge amount of embedded safety critical computer software. Neither did any major business suffer any

A Systematic Introduction to Change Management

(publicized) downtime or interruption to their customers relating to Y2K.

Further Information:

1. Was Y2K a costly non-event?

http://www.computerweekly.com/feature/Was-Y2K-a-costly-non-event

2. National Geographical — Y2K bug.

http://nationalgeographic.org/encyclopedia/Y2K-bug/

3. Y2K: Money Well Spent?

http://www.everything2000.com/news/computer/y2kmoneywellspent.asp

Reader Exercise

- Review the '12 Principles of Change Management' earlier in the book.
- Check out the further information section above on this change.
- How successful do you consider this change to be?
- Identify at least 3 things which the change leaders got right.
- Identify at least 1 thing the leaders could have done much better.
- Compare your answers with my opinions on the change at the end of this chapter

A Systematic Introduction to Change Management

The Good Friday Agreement (N. Ireland Peace Process)

The Challenge:

Northern Ireland had been mired in sectarian violence and political stalemate since the early 1970's. However, in July 1997 the IRA restored their ceasefire and, by September of that year, the political representatives of the republican and loyalist paramilitaries were engaged in the talks at Stormont in Belfast with the objective of coming up with a political solution which all parties could sell to their communities.

The Results:

The Good Friday Agreement (aka The Belfast Agreement) came into force in December 1998 when Northern Ireland's politicians took their seats at the local assembly. However, it would not be plain sailing. The devolved government only returned to Northern Ireland in 2007 in a government of political extremes. The loyalist DUP's Ian Paisley became First Minister and republican Sinn Féin's Martin McGuinness the Deputy First Minister.

According to the BBC:

'It was a political alignment of polar opposites that would have been unimaginable in 1998 and a sign of just how far Northern Ireland had come from the darkest days of the Troubles'.

A Systematic Introduction to Change Management

Further Information:

1. BBC History Channel.

http://www.bbc.co.uk/history/events/good_friday_agreement

2. The Belfast Agreement, The Northern Ireland Office, 10 April 1998.

https://www.gov.uk/government/publications/the-belfast-agreement

3. The Good Friday Agreement – An Overview, Democratic Progress Institute, June 2003.

http://www.democraticprogress.org/wp-content/uploads/2013/07/The-Good-Friday-Agreement-An-Overview.pdf

Reader Exercise

- Review the '12 Principles of Change Management' earlier in the book.
- Check out the further information section above on this change.
- How successful do you consider this change to be?
- Identify at least 3 things which the change leaders got right.
- Identify at least 1 thing the leaders could have done much better.
- Compare your answers with my opinions on the change at the end of this chapter.

A Systematic Introduction to Change Management

Smoking in Public Places (England)

The Challenge:

Second-hand smoke is the combination of smoke from the burning end of a cigarette and the smoke exhaled by smokers. You can be exposed to second-hand smoke in homes, cars, the workplace, and public places, such as bars, restaurants, and recreational settings. There is no safe exposure level to second-hand smoke.

Because studies show that laws banning smoking in public places help improve worker and customer health, many countries such as England were considering introducing laws making workplaces, public places, restaurants, and bars smoke-free.

The Results:

A smoking ban in England, making it illegal to smoke in all enclosed workplaces in England, came into force on 1 July 2007 as a consequence of the Health Act 2006. Similar bans had already been introduced by the rest of the United Kingdom before this — Scotland on 26 March 2006, Wales on 2 April 2007 and Northern Ireland on 30 April 2007.

A Systematic Introduction to Change Management

Further Information:

1. Smoking ban's impact five years on, BBC News, July 2012.

http://www.bbc.co.uk/news/health-18628811

2. Smoking ban has saved 40,000 lives, The Independent, 29 June 2008.

http://www.independent.co.uk/life-style/health-and-families/health-news/smoking-ban-has-saved-40000-lives-856885.html

3. Ten years on from the smoking ban: Was it the right decision? STV News, March 2016.

http://stv.tv/news/scotland/1347576-ten-years-on-from-the-smoking-ban-was-it-the-right-decision/

Reader Exercise

- Review the '12 Principles of Change Management' earlier in the book.
- Check out the further information section above on this change.
- How successful do you consider this change to be?
- Identify at least 3 things which the change leaders got right.
- Identify at least 1 thing the leaders could have done much better.
- Compare your answers with my opinions on the change at the end of this chapter.

A Systematic Introduction to Change Management

JC Penney

The Challenge:

The year was 2012, and rather than offer sales and coupons, JC Penney, the 111-year-old US retailer, had a better idea: "month-long values" that would do away with the hype and drama of specials and so-called "reductions." Instead, consumers could rest assured they were always getting the best price.

The Results:

Unfortunately, customers hated the idea and criticized JCP's implementation. The company suffered a 20% drop in profits in the first quarter of 2012, along with strong negative consumer feedback. JCP's then-president, Michael Francis, announced his resignation soon thereafter.

A Systematic Introduction to Change Management

Further Information:

1. JC Penney's Epic Rebranding Fail, *Forbes Magazine*, June 2012.

http://www.forbes.com/sites/marketshare/2012/06/15/jc-penneys-epic-rebranding-fail/

2. The JC Penney debacle: Where did Johnson go wrong? *Retail Customer Experience*, March 2013.

http://www.retailcustomerexperience.com/articles/the-jc-penney-debacle-where-did-johnson-go-wrong/

3. What Went Wrong at J.C. Penney? Harvard Business School, August 2013.

http://hbswk.hbs.edu/item/what-went-wrong-at-j-c-penney

Reader Exercise

- Review the '12 Principles of Change Management' earlier in the book.
- Check out the further information section above on this change.
- How successful do you consider this change to be?
- Identify at least 3 things which the change leaders got right.
- Identify at least 1 thing the leaders could have done much better.
- Compare your answers with my opinions on the change at the end of this chapter.

A Systematic Introduction to Change Management

Ford Motor Company

The Challenge:

When new CEO Alan Mulally took over the Ford Motor Company in September 2006, the company was badly broken. Its stock price had fallen precipitously (the low was $1.01 a share in 2008), its debt was at "junk" status, and 2006 would go down as the worst year in its history with a $12.7 billion loss. It was widely expected that Ford would eventually file for bankruptcy.

The Results:

In October 2011, Ford Motor Company were able to report that it was profitable again in the third quarter, earning $1.65 billion — the tenth consecutive profitable quarter! The company also reported that it secured a new labor contract with the United Automobile Workers union and said it was close to restoring a dividend to shareholders that was slashed during Ford's hard times.

A Systematic Introduction to Change Management

Further Information:

1. Ford Motor Company Turnaround: 5 Lessons for Emerging from Hard Times, *International Business Times*, 2011.

   http://www.ibtimes.com/ford-motor-company-turnaround-5-lessons-emerging-hard-times-212580

2. How Ford CEO Alan Mullaly turned a broken company into the industry's comeback kid, Harry Kraemer Kellogg School of Management, June 2015.

   http://qz.com/431078/how-ford-ceo-alan-mullaly-turned-a-broken-company-into-the-industrys-comeback-kid/

3. Ford's Alan Mulally – Effective Change Agent of the Present Day, *Research Methodology*, February 2013.

   http://research-methodology.net/fords-alan-mulally-effective-change-agent-of-the-present-day/

Reader Exercise

- Review the '12 Principles of Change Management' earlier in the book.
- Check out the further information section above on this change.
- How successful do you consider this change to be?
- Identify at least 3 things which the change leaders got right.
- Identify at least 1 thing the leaders could have done much better.
- Compare your answers with my opinions on the change at the end of this chapter.

A Systematic Introduction to Change Management

5 Featured Change Projects: Perspectives

Y2K (The Millennium Bug)

Things they got right

- The narrative about the need to address the problem and the potentially dire consequences of ignoring it.

- Success in influencing the top people in organizations who could find the huge budgets necessary to fund the extra work.

- The need to start the work much earlier than the layman would have understood – leaving it until 1999 would be too late.

Things they could have done better

- They oversold the impact of the problem resulting in a feeling afterward that organizations probably spent 2-3 times more than they actually needed to. This left a sense in many organizations about being ruthlessly exploited by the very people who caused the problem in the first place (IT).

- They failed to create any positive story about the change – it was pure 'burning platform' whereas there could also have been a story about technology refresh or platform modernization.

A Systematic Introduction to Change Management

The Good Friday Agreement (XE "The N. Ireland Peace Process"**)**

Things they got right

- Creating a change story which had a core shared narrative but enough wiggle room in the margins for the politicians on both sides of the political divide to sell it to their constituencies as a 'victory.'

- The support of high-profile supporters such as Bill Clinton, Tony Blair, Bertie Ahern and Irish Americans.

- Turning some potential opponents on the paramilitary side of politics into supporters before embarking on the change.

Things they could have done better

- A key objective was to bring the extremists on both sides into the peace process but this was felt by many to be at the expense of the moderates on both sides of the political divide. This is evidenced by the fact the two main moderate parties are now much smaller and have many fewer MPs in the local assembly than the two hard-line parties.

A Systematic Introduction to Change Management

Smoking in Public Places (England)

Things they got right

- Creating a compelling story for the change, particularly drawing on examples elsewhere and strong medical evidence.

- Recognition from the outset that there would be serious opposition from the Tobacco and Hospitality industries.

- Having a clear and unambiguous implementation plan and schedule about what would happen by when.

Things they could have done better

- Creating a change story that was seen as too dogmatic, no compromise and overly driven by healthcare resulting in the complaint that numerous pubs (1200 in England) had to close with the resulting job losses. Also the sense that 'freedom of choice' was trampled on.

JC Penney

Things they got right

- They understood the compelling and urgent need for some kind of dramatic change to the retailer if it was to compete and survive.

Things they could have done better

- The story and benefits of the change were weak to the target audience.
- They underestimated the attractiveness of the 'Sale Culture' with their customer base.
- They tried to make a major change to consumer behavior without adequate research, testing, tuning and piloting.

A Systematic Introduction to
Change Management

Ford Motor Company

Things they got right

- They really engaged their key stakeholders with the story of the change.

- The CEO had a great hands-on communication style and a positive and optimistic approach to the inevitable problems.

- They were prepared to take calculated risks.

Things they could have done better

- They could have started sooner!

A Systematic Introduction to Change Management

Other Major Change Projects

Projects

Shell 2004, Santander 2008, Direct Line 2008.

Reference

http://www.managers.org.uk/insights/news/2015/july/the-5-greatest-examples-of-change-management-in-business-history

Projects

British Airways, California State University.

Reference

http://www.brighthubpm.com/change-management/55056-examples-of-change-management-plans-that-worked/

Projects

Successes: Altassian (Software), Pearson (Publishing).

Failures: Walmart (Retail), Borders (Bookstore).

Reference

https://www.tinypulse.com/blog/sk-successful-organizational-change-examples

A Systematic Introduction to Change Management

Projects

Yahoo (Online), California State University, British Airways.

Reference

https://www.tinypulse.com/blog/3-examples-of-organizational-change-and-why-they-got-it-right

Projects

Shell, Santander, Target (Retailer), Abercrombie and Fitch (Clothing), Apple.

Reference

http://change.walkme.com/5-oscar-worthy-examples-of-change-management-in-business-history/

Projects

Coca Cola.

Reference

http://ivythesis.typepad.com/term_paper_topics/2009/09/change-management-in-coca-cola-corporation.html

Projects

Blackberry (cell phones).

Reference

https://bvonderlinn.wordpress.com/2013/08/02/managing-transitions-real-life-examples-part-1/

Projects

TrueLocal.com.au (Online Business Directory).

Reference

http://www.academia.edu/2369683/Case_Study_Analysis_on_an_Organisation_Change_Management_and_Change_Process

Projects

VF (Clothing), Nokia (Telecoms).

Reference

https://www.bcgperspectives.com/content/articles/transformation_change_management_five_case_studies_transformation_excellence/

A Systematic Introduction to Change Management

SELECT READING LIST ON CHANGE

Leading Change: Why Transformation Efforts Fail
JOHN P. KOTTER.

Managing Change: The Art of Balancing
JEANIE DANIEL DUCK.

Successful Change Programs Begin with Results
ROBERT H. SCHAFFER AND HARVEY A. THOMSON.

See also my blog (www.bioteams.com) for a collection of articles on Change Management *tagged* 'Change Management'.

APPENDICES

A Systematic Introduction to Change Management

Appendix 1: Introduction to Business Cases

The Purpose and Structure of a Business Case

Along with the Change Narrative, there should also be a Business Case which estimates the costs and the benefits of the proposed change. This should have been produced before the change management plan but if it has not been or it is inadequate you will need to revisit it.

It is very important not to forget that the Change Management Project is not 'The Project' it is only the, albeit vital, part of 'The Project' which supports the necessary changes to ensure 'The Project' is a success.

'The Project' could be a major technology implementation such as a new corporate ERP system or a new global videoconferencing system. It could also be the merging of operations with a newly acquired company or the introduction of new working practices across the company.

According to 'The Business Case Checklist' [1] which is an excellent short (46-page) booklet and a good investment in itself there are 12 key questions you should consider when making a major investment, often with a technology aspect to it:

1. What is the business need?
2. What is the investment that addresses the business need?
3. What technology underlies the investment?
4. What are the benefits of the investment?
5. What are the costs of the investment?

A Systematic Introduction to Change Management

6. What are the major risks?
7. How did we value the investment?
8. Is the investment feasible and a good fit?
9. What alternatives did we consider?
10. How do we execute on the investment?
11. Is this a good business case?
12. Do we invest?

Each of these 12 topics can be broken down into a number of sub-questions, for example:

1. *What is the business need?*
- Is the Business Need Clear and Understood?
- Is the Business Need Acute?
- What is the complication which makes the status quo unbearable?
- Why solve this problem now?

Interestingly the checklist above does not ask the obvious question 'What Change Management will be required' however you should have already addressed this in your Change Management Plan!

*A Systematic Introduction to
Change Management*

Key Business Case Calculations

There are a number of different calculations [2] associated with Business Cases including. The most common are:

Net Benefits: the total benefits <u>less</u> the total costs to achieve those benefits.

Return on Investment (RoI): the ratio of the net benefits to the total costs expressed as a percentage.

Payback (or Breakeven) Period: the time taken for the total benefits gained to become equal to the total costs invested.

Net Present Value (NPV)*: an investment calculation which discounts by an annual rate to take into account the reality that money tomorrow is less valuable than money today. Also known as **Discounted Cash Flow (DCF).**

Internal Rate of Return (IRR)*: is the annual discount rate which would make the NPV equal to zero. Effectively the bank interest you would need on the money to match your project return.

NOTE
If you do need to use NPV or IRR, be careful to base your final decision on NPV not IRR. IRR is easier to understand and good for discussion but does not give you absolute value, and does not take into account the number of years for which the return is earned.

A Systematic Introduction to Change Management

A SIMPLE WORKED EXAMPLE

Imagine we invest £100 in Year 0 and get £50 back each year for 3 years…….

Net Benefits = (3* £50) - £100 = £50

Return on Investment (RoI) = 100*(£50/£100) = 50%

Payback (or Breakeven) Period = 2 Years

Net Present Value (NPV):
At an annual discount rate of 8%
PV = 50/ $(1.08)^1$ + 50/ $(1.08)^2$ + 50/ $(1.08)^3$ = £129
NPV = £129 - £100 = £29

Note the difference between the Net Benefits and the NPV!

Internal Rate of Return (IRR):
The annual discount rate which would make the NPV equal to zero – in this case about 23%. Note the actual calculation requires an IRR calculator (many available free on the web and on traditional calculators)

References

1. *The Business Case Checklist: Everything You Need to Review a Business Case, Avoid Failed Projects, and Turn Technology into ROI*, Business Case Pro.
2. *Financial Intelligence – A Managers Guide to knowing what the numbers really mean*, Harvard Business Press, Berman and Knight, 2006.

Chapter 6 (pp 177–196), 'How to calculate (and really understand) Return on Investment' is particularly relevant

*A Systematic Introduction to
Change Management*

Appendix 2: Lite Framework for Change Mgt.

The late Stephen Covey always reminded us that "the main thing was to keep the main thing the main thing!"

However, when you think about "Change Management" you could be excused for thinking it's all about detailed road maps and large tomes of procedures and checklists.

These are all important but sometimes they can also sadly distract from the whole point of the exercise.

To stop you falling into this trap I offer you my easy-to-remember, 4-point mental checklist based on the human body to help you constantly check that you have not been "detail distracted!"

The Head, Hearts, Hands & Feet Model of Change

1. *HEAD*

Is there a compelling reason for change — merely a good reason for change is not enough? The term "burning platform" comes to mind. By not changing you must be exposing your enterprise to a major threat or walking away from a major opportunity.

There must be a sound economic reason for change which can be succinctly and clearly articulated and accepted by the leaders of the enterprise.

A Systematic Introduction to Change Management

2.   HEART

Heart is all about the "appetite" for change in the key leaders. I have seen so many change initiatives with great HEAD flounder because the key leaders did not want it enough or thought that a compelling reason was somehow enough. Unlike HEAD, HEART is an ongoing challenge — you need to establish it in the first place and then keep it alive until the change is truly bedded in.

So how do you establish it? The first step is, through frank 1:1 conversations, to establish the individual appetite of the key leaders. This needs to be done sensitively as the objective is not to sign the leaders all up but to find out where they really are!

3.   HANDS and FEET

If you have the HEAD and the HEART, then you need the How and the Who. This is where the HANDS and FEET come in. HANDS concerns how the change will be brought about. In a nutshell, HANDS is about the plan for the new processes, systems, incentives, practices, success measures and required behavior changes. Does the plan or proposed plan cover all the bases? Is the work already done an adequate basis for change or will it need to be reworked or binned?

Finally, the FEET, or HEELS if you simply must have alliteration, represents the feet on the ground to manage the change. I have never yet seen a change successfully delivered without a competent project manager working to a public and serious deadline the achievement of which is linked to their personal performance review and

A Systematic Introduction to Change Management

remuneration and with adequate personal time and access to additional resources as required to make it happen.

So to ensure you don't forget the whole point of change management as you wade through the detail just remember your own body and your 4 vital organs and limbs — HEAD, HEART, HANDS and FEET!

Appendix 3: TechVet Company Briefing

1. *Company Background*

TechVet designs and manufactures ultrasound equipment and is a world leader in bovine and ovine pregnancy detection.

Since 1980 TechVet has been designing, manufacturing and distributing its own range of products dedicated to farm animal applications and improving animal care using ultrasound diagnosis. TechVet's product range is well known for high quality, portability, and ease of use.

A world leader in bovine ultrasound scanning equipment, TechVet is focused on supplying bespoke products and services as well as becoming a global partner that customers, distributors and suppliers can rely on.

Based in the UK and the USA and with a worldwide distribution network (currently 37 distributors), TechVet's business goal is to exceed customer needs and expectations through innovative products and professional customer service.

2. *Services & Products*

Main Service Areas
- Breeding Animals
- Farm Inputs (Feed additives, Seed, Veterinary medicine products)

A Systematic Introduction to Change Management

- Husbandry and feeding techniques

Main Product Lines

- Digital X-Ray
- X-Ray Machines and Generators
- Ultrasound
- Image Management

4. *Financial Position*

TechVet has 3 main markets – UK and Europe, The Americas and Asia.

The UK and Europe contribute 60% of the revenue but the market is static and profit margins are around 12%. The Americas contribute 30% of the revenue with the market growing at 5% per annum and profit margins at around 10%. Asia contributes the balance of revenue, however, this market is growing at 15% per annum and profit margins are in excess of 20%.

5. *Business Priorities*

TechVet's current view of its top 4 business priorities for the next 12-24 months are:

<u>Distributor Growth</u>

- particularly finding suitable new partners in Asia

<u>Cost reduction in European markets</u>

- to address profit pressures

Staff Recruitment and Retention

- particularly staff willing to travel internationally

New Product Development

- broadening beyond hardware by developing Imaging Services revenue with an initial focus on Europe

These could of course change at any point!

6. *The ERP Project*

To date, the company has relied upon homegrown IT to handle its Sales Order Processing, Production Control, Warehousing and Distribution. The business is growing rapidly with typically a new distributor every month and the product range is also expanding. The current system is creaking at the seams and is particularly tricky to change or add new products or distributors.

A robust new IT infrastructure has been successfully implemented along with a new set of financial systems. The priority is now to implement a professional ERP (Enterprise Resource Planning) system across the company which would be accessible by all staff and have appropriate controls for distributors to check on their orders.

7. *Your Role in the Project*

You joined the company from University 10 years ago with a Business and Technology degree on the company

A Systematic Introduction to Change Management

graduate intake. During your time here you have been given the opportunity to operate in a number of different areas of the business, including some management responsibilities.

As a final test of whether you are ready for "something more senior" you have been asked to become project manager for the ERP project reporting directly to Heather Hunt (Operations Director). Heather has told you (off the record) that whilst on paper she will be project sponsor, it is really "your baby" as she has a full workload and (privately) wonders if this is the best time to be putting in an ERP system with everything else that is going on in the company.

You have recruited an internal team of part-timers to support you and have 2 full-time external consultants. The company has already selected the SAP ERP system and fully budgeted for its costs plus the costs of the two external consultants (for 1 year). You have been told that a 'pilot system' has to be implemented successfully in 9 months. The scope of such a pilot is not yet defined.

8.   Tech Vet Organizational Structure

The Tech Vet Executive team and wider director group are represented in the org. chart overleaf. **You report into Heather.**

A Systematic Introduction to Change Management

[Organizational chart showing: Diane Dobson (Chief Executive) at top; reporting to her: Andre Anderson (Sales & Marketing Director), Jane Jacobs (Finance & IT Director), Garth Gordon (Operations & Production Director). Under Andre Anderson: Frank Frazer (Sales Director), Bev Brown (Marketing Director), Ed Eagle (S&M Admin Director). Under Garth Gordon: Helen Hunt (Operations Director), Ike Ingram (Production Director), Carol Crooks (Logistics Director).]

9. ERP References

1. *Enterprise Resource Planning,* Wikipedia.
https://en.wikipedia.org/wiki/Enterprise_resource_planning

2. *SAP - ERP Introduction,* SAP.
http://www.tutorialspoint.com/sap/sap_introduction.htm

3. *The Five Challenges of Change Management in an ERP Project,* PCubed.
http://www.pcubed.com/bulletins/five-challenges-change-management-erp-project

4. *Five Change Management Strategies for Global ERP Implementations,* Panorama.
http://panorama-consulting.com/five-change-management-strategies-for-global-erp-implementations/

A Systematic Introduction to Change Management

Appendix 4: High Performing Teams in a hurry!

Can you create a High-Performing Team in a day or afternoon or even over lunch? Of course not! However, if you are put in the position where you, as a leader, must get the very best out of a group of colleagues in very short timescales what can you do? **This is frequent change management challenge for leaders.** Here is my 4-step approach to 'Instant Team'.

STEP1: Create Team 'Game Plan'

Below is my 7-point checklist which teams can use to produce a Team Game Plan (1-2 pages maximum):

1.   **R**oles
How will we divide up the team responsibilities?
2.   **A**greements (Ground Rules)
How will we deal with each other as colleagues and team members?
3.   **P**rocesses/Practices
What are the 2-3 most important team processes/practices will we put in place and follow?
4.   **P**riorities
How will we decide what is most important, particularly in dilemmas or under pressure? [2]
5.   **O**rganizational Values
What values are the most important to us as a team?
6.   **R**esults
What specific results must we achieve as our minimum team performance level?
7.   **T**argets
What is our 'stretch' target, our ambition to exceed our minimum performance level?

The first letter of each element spells 'R.A.P.P.O.R.T.' which is a useful mnemonic for a Team Game Plan. This is apt as 'Rapport' can be defined as *'A close and harmonious relationship in which the groups concerned understand each other's feelings or ideas and communicate well'* according to THE OXFORD DICTIONARY.

STEP 2: Test the Team

Do some short team-based activity as a Team and try to follow your Team Game Plan. You need to set aside at least 1 hour but 3 hours is better. If you have 3 hours, you can play a team-based business simulation or even some off-site activity. If you only have 1 hour you can still have a team problem-solving brainstorming meeting on a practical topic with which everyone is already familiar.

STEP 3: Reflect and Improve

At the end of this team activity, team members should take at least 30 minutes to discuss and reflect on a small number of key questions typically:

- How well are we working as a team – what could we improve?
- What would we do differently if we did the activity again?
- How closely are we following our team game plan – does this need to be revised?

If you have 2-3 hours, then you can conduct this review more than once as this allows the team to see visible improvements quickly. Another very useful device is to have the teams self-assess against the '*7 Mistakes Teams Make Under Pressure*' (see overleaf).

A Systematic Introduction to Change Management

The '7 mistakes' have been gathered over ten years and represent the most common mistakes teams make participating in team-based business simulation games.

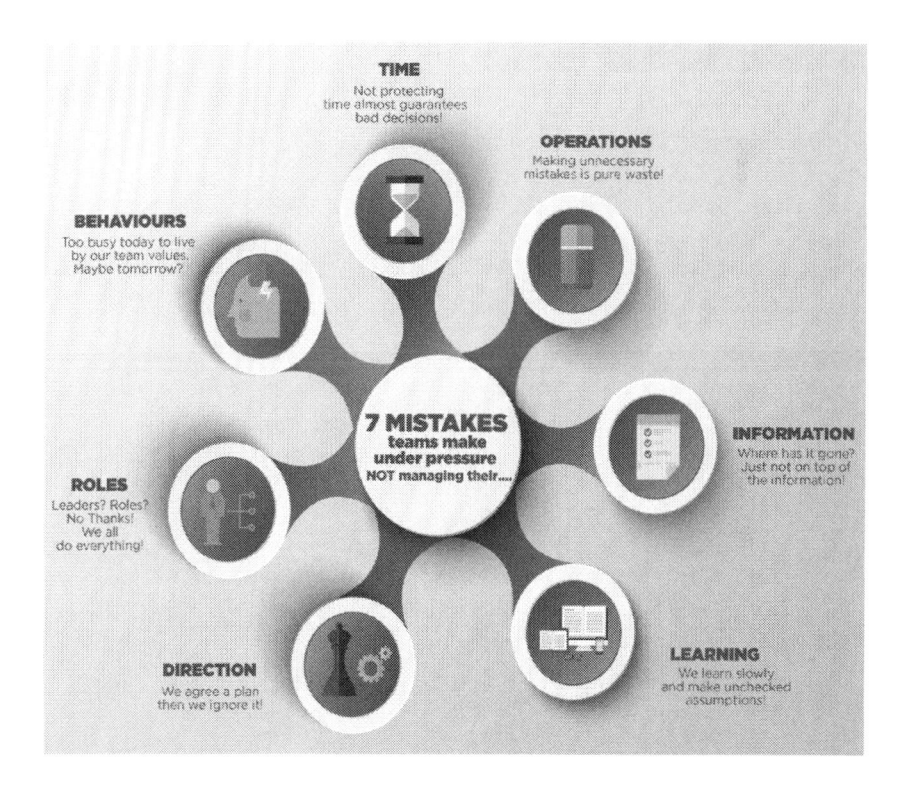

TIME
Not protecting time almost guarantees bad decisions!

OPERATIONS
Making unnecessary mistakes is pure waste!

BEHAVIOURS
Too busy today to live by our team values. Maybe tomorrow?

INFORMATION
Where has it gone? Just not on top of the information!

ROLES
Leaders? Roles? No Thanks! We all do everything!

DIRECTION
We agree a plan then we ignore it!

LEARNING
We learn slowly and make unchecked assumptions!

7 MISTAKES teams make under pressure NOT managing their....

STEP 4: Execute and Review

Now you need to direct the team to the job in hand with the specific extra directive of 'Follow your Game Plan!' In addition, you must build in a regular (e.g. weekly) review cycle where you repeat the self-reflection/improvement from Step 4 using, of course, all the other guidance and tools offered in the rest of the book!

A Systematic Introduction to Change Management

The Evolution of Team Working

If you observe newly formed and existing teams playing business simulations and other intensive challenges, you can gain some important insights into how team-working actually 'evolves'. This knowledge can help you accelerate the evolution of effective team working and collaboration in your own organizational teams.

On the road to Effective Team Collaboration there seems to be two intermediate phases of 'naïve collaboration' which teams often seem to go through - *Hyper-Communication* and *Over-Delegation*.

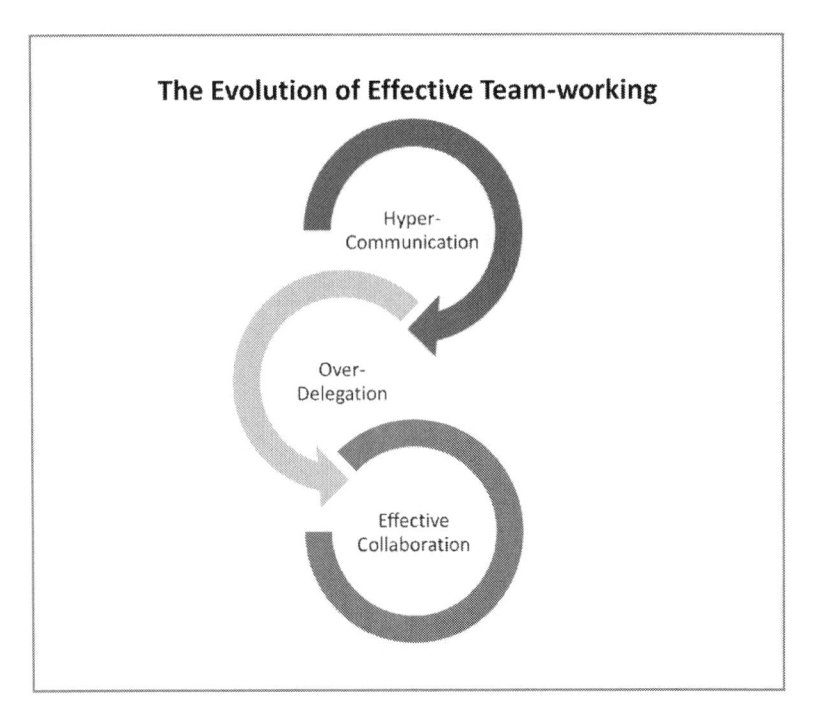

The Evolution of Effective Team-working

- Hyper-Communication
- Over-Delegation
- Effective Collaboration

A Systematic Introduction to Change Management

PHASE 1: Hyper-Communication

In this phase almost every team member is involved in almost every team conversation. It is very democratic and feels really good but the problem is that it just takes forever. A team operating like this will not hit its deadlines.

An organisational team meeting which conducts its Operational Meetings like this will not get through its agenda. In my experience teams usually start here on their journey towards effective collaboration. Teams in this phase genuinely believe that they are collaborating well UNTIL they suddenly discover that working like this is just not practical as it simply takes too long!

When teams have tried 'Hyper-Communication' they often *over-correct* and move to the next phase of naive collaboration: 'Over-Delegation'.

PHASE 2: Over-Delegation

In this phase the team quickly agree that they need to work faster and more efficiently. To achieve this, they wisely decide that they need some roles and division of labour but they 'over-delegate'. By this I mean they give out jobs to the different members and sub-teams but do not support this with sufficient communications to ensure they all stay on the same page.

Like the first phase, Hyper-Communication, teams think they have fixed their collaboration and they feel they are being very efficient UNTIL they discover, typically near the end of the round, that they are no longer all on the same page and that the team members have been working to different assumptions and priorities which invalidates much of their good work.

PHASE 3: Effective Collaboration

Once teams have experienced both of these naïve forms of collaboration (Hyper-Communication and Over-Delegation) they are well placed to find a middle ground with represents Effective Collaboration.

As with Over-Delegation they allocate roles but this time they also ensure that this is supported by on-going communications particularly around task objectives and early review of provisional findings/decisions before they become finalised.

Accelerated Team Development

From these insights it is clear that many teams find it very difficult to move directly into Effective Collaboration without first experiencing **and learning** from both Hyper-Communication and Over-Delegation.

I can't prove it but feel strongly that it may also be the case that many organizational teams simply *flip-flop* between the two naïve collaboration phases of Hyper-Communication and Over-Delegation without ever making the break-through into Effective Collaboration … perhaps all the time believing, they are already doing it!

A Systematic Introduction to Change Management

Therefore, to fast track effective team-working you need 3 simple ingredients:

1. **Mechanisms such as competitive business simulation games** or other short team challenges.

2. **Briefing for the teams on the challenges with specific deadlines and goals** but without any instruction about how they are to behave other than that they are a team.

3. **Facilitated team self-analysis sessions at the end of each round** or chunk of work to let teams review what kind of collaboration they are employing and how they might improve it.

If you carefully and skilfully work with these 3 ingredients, you can help teams in your organization develop effective team-working and collaboration skills in a much faster timescale than might be possible using other methods.

===
This section is a short extract from book 1 in The Systematic Guide series: 'A Systematic Guide to High Performing Teams (HPTs).
===

INDEX

7 Mistakes Teams Make Under Pressure 146
70% Failure Rate..........26
Accelerated Team Development............150
Adoption Model 96
Agent-Based Simulation 81
AIDCA Model 95
Alan Mulally.................121
Albert-László Barabási .91
Ambivalence.................62
Apollo 13........................32
Attitude 61
Balanced Scorecard 27
Behavioural Economics 104
Best Practice Sharing ...76
Betweenness.................69
Biological Model of Change 24
Bottlenecks....................70
Bounded Rationality ..104
Brokers 70
Burning Platform..........51
Business Case 133
Bystanders.....................70
CASH Model.................38
Change Champion ..41, 60
Change Diffusion Model 83
Change Engagement Model.........................58

Change Narratives 51
Change Opponents 40
Change Plan......35, 36, 54
Change Planning Checklist 55
Change Planning Simulation 83
Change Simulation Game 80
Change Supporters.......39
Charles Spinosa........8, 62
Closeness......................69
Cognitive Dissonance .106
COHORT.......................80
Community Change Visualisation 76
Confirmation Bias 104
Core Principles 35
Crossing The Chasm 48
Data Protection 98
Degrees Centrality........69
DICE Assessment 71
Early Adopters 48
Effective Collaboration 150
Evolution of Team Working 148
Experiential and Social learning 81
Fast Track Effective Team-Working 151
Force Field Analysis.....49

152

Ford Motor Company 112, 121, 122, 127
Friendly Lightweight....63
Fritjof Capra..................24
Geoffrey Moore 49
Getting to Yes...............101
Golden Opportunity.....52
Head, Hearts & Hands Model 137
Herd Behaviour 107
Hyper-Communication 148, 149, 150
ICE Model 49
Indirect Interventions..42
Infection Model............47
Influence 35, 39, 41, 61, 62, 63, 66, 68
Insight...........................61
Intrinsic Connectivity ..70
Investment Calculations 135
JC Penney 112, 119, 120, 126
John Kotter.......27, 30, 37
Lagging Indicators 28
Leading Indicators.......28
Lewin Model.................49
Maslow's Hierarchy of Needs 52
Maturity Model 76
Michael Hammer 27
Microsoft Excel 68
Net Benefits.........135, 136
Net Present Value (NPV) 135
New Habits Model........47

NodeXL 68
Operational Meetings.149
Organizational Influence 39, 41, 63, 64, 66, 81
Over-Delegation 148, 149, 150
Payback (or Breakeven) Period 135
PDCA Cycle.................109
Perturbation Management 25, 110
Political Model of Change 22
Presuasion 102
Principled Negotiation 101
R.A.P.P.O.R.T. 146
Return on Investment 135, 136
Risk................................94
River Diagram 76
Robert Cialdini 102
Secret Guru 63
Simulation 146, 148
Smoking in Public Places 112, 117, 125
SNA 66, 68, 69, 70
Social Influence 40, 41, 63, 64, 69, 81
Social Network Analysis 68, 90
SPREAD 83
Stages of Grief Model...48
Stakeholder Analysis....39
Stakeholder Map....39, 62
Story of the Change 35, 36
Super-Connectors.........91

A Systematic Introduction to Change Management

Team Game Plan 145
TechVet..........53, 140, 141
The Good Friday Agreement112, 115, 116, 124
The Hard Side of Change Management 71
The N. Ireland Peace Process..............112, 115

Two Types of Change ...26
Understanding43, 46, 57, 59
Unfreeze - Freeze Model 49
Visionaries 48
Word of Mouth.............86
Y2K (The Millennium Bug)...........112, 113, 123

A Systematic Introduction to Change Management

Your Own Notes (1)

*A Systematic Introduction to
Change Management*

Your Own Notes (2)

A Systematic Introduction to Change Management

Your Own Notes (3)

Printed in Poland
by Amazon Fulfillment
Poland Sp. z o.o., Wrocław